W9-CUL-799

INITIAL
PUBLIC
OFFERING

INITIAL
PUBLIC
OFFERING

Richard P. Kleeburg, C.M.A., M.B.A., J.D., Ph.D.

Australia · Canada · Mexico · Singapore · Spain · United Kingdom · United States

Initial Public Offering
Richard P. Kleeburg, C.M.A., M.B.A., J.D., Ph.D.

COPYRIGHT© 2005 Texere, an imprint of Thomson/South-Western, a part of The Thomson Corporation. Thomson and the Star logo are trademarks used herein under license.

Composed by: Chip Butzko

Printed in the United States of America by R.R. Donnelley, Crawfordsville
1 2 3 4 5 08 07 06 05
This book is printed on acid-free paper.

ISBN: 0-324-20056-0

This publication is designed to provide accurate and authoritative information in regard to the subject matter covered. It is sold with the understanding that the publisher is not engaged in rendering legal, accounting or other professional services. If expert assistance is required, the services of a competent professional person should be sought.

ALL RIGHTS RESERVED. No part of this work covered by the copyright hereon may be reproduced or used in any form or by any means—graphic, electronic, or mechanical, including photocopying, recording, taping, Web distribution, or information storage and retrieval systems, or in any other manner—without the written permission of the publisher.

The names of all companies or products mentioned herein are used for identification purposes only and may be trademarks or registered trademarks of their respective owners. Texere disclaims any affiliation, association, connection with, sponsorship, or endorsements by such owners.

For permission to use material from this text or product, submit a request online at http://www.thomsonrights.com.

Library of Congress Cataloging in Publication Number is available. See page 243 for details.

For more information about our products, contact us at:

Thomson Learning Academic Resource Center
1-800-423-0563

Thomson HigherEducation
5191 Natorp Boulevard
Mason, Ohio 45040
USA

Asia (including India)
Thomson Learning
5 Shenton Way
#01-01 UIC Building
Singapore 068808

Australia/New Zealand
Thomson Learning Australia
102 Dodds Street
Southbank, Victoria 3006
Australia

Canada
Thomson Nelson
1120 Birchmount Road
Toronto, Ontario
M1K 5G4
Canada

Latin America
Thomson Learning
Seneca, 53
Colonia Polanco
11560 Mexico
D.F. Mexico

UK/Europe/Middle East/Africa
Thomson Learning
High Holborn House
50/51 Bedford Row
London WC1R 4LR
United Kingdom

Spain (including Portugal)
Thomson Paraninfo
Calle Magallanes, 25
28015 Madrid, Spain

Other Titles Available from
TEXERE

The Financial Troubleshooter, Jae K. Shim, 0-324-20648-8

Process to Profits: Strategic Planning for the Growing Business, William Lasher, 0-324-22387-0

Cargo in Jeopardy: Securing Each Link in the Supply Chain, Edward Badolato, 0-324-22284-X

Preventative Law for Business Professionals, Martin E. Segal, 0-324-22574-1

Growing Your Business Globally, Robert A. Taft, 0-324-20303-9

The Escher Cycle: Creating Self-Reinforcing Business Advantage, Finn Jackson, 1-58799-194-2

Earnings Management: An Executive Perspective, Thomas E. McKee, 0-324-22325-0

Frontline HR: A Handbook for the Emerging Manager, Jeffery S. Hornsby and Donald F. Kuratko, 0-324-20322-3

Higher Profits through Customer Lock-In, Joachim Bueschken, 0-324-20265-2

Up Against the Retail Giants, A. Coskun Samli, 0-324-23308-6

The Export Marketing Imperative, Michael R. Czinkota, Illkka Ronkainen, and Marta Ortiz-Buonafina, 0-324-22258-0

Triumph from Failure: Lessons from Life for Business Success, Alistair McAlpine, 1-58799-181-0

The Art of the Advantage: 36 Strategies to Seize the Competitive Edge, Kaihan Krippendorf, 1-58799-168-3

Entering and Succeeding in Emerging Countries: Marketing to the Forgotten Majority, A. Coskun Samli, 0-538-72698-9

Finance Just in Time: Understanding the Key to Business and Investment Before It's Too Late, Hugo Dixon, 1-58799-149-7

Inside Washington: Government Resources for International Business, William A. Delphos, 0-538-72692-X

Find these Texere titles and more at: www.thomson.com/learning/texere

TABLE OF CONTENTS

ABOUT THE AUTHOR

Richard Paul Kleeburg, C.M.A., M.B.A., J.D., Ph.D., is vice president/controller at Pan American Band FSB in Newport Beach, California. Previously he was senior audit manager with Deloitte & Touche and manager of accounting with Crown Bolt.

Dr. Kleeburg was honored in the 2003-2004 "Who's Who" in *Finance Business*, is a lifetime member of Beta Alpha Psi, Cal Poly Pomona, and is a dean's list scholar at Cal Poly Pomona and the University of California, Santa Barbara.

He has in excess of 15 years experience in accounting and finance. His expertise lies in corporate financial planning and analysis. Dr. Kleeburg is a frequent speaker on accounting and finance issues at numerous colleges throughout the Untied States. In addition, he has been the lead consultant and co-consultant on numerous IPO offerings throughout his career.

CHAPTER 1

INTRODUCTION

An initial public offering (IPO) is the process many business owners go through in the hope of becoming extremely wealthy. What many do not understand, though, is that with the large profits that may be earned come large sacrifices in terms of time and control that must be made.

As I will stress repeatedly throughout this book, the IPO marks the beginning of a process, not the end. Many successful private companies would have been much better off remaining private instead of going public. There are numerous demands on new public companies, such as giving the public financial information that used to remain private, or having to go through annual audits to ensure the new shareholders that the company's accounting records are properly stated.

Still, while taking a private company public entails a huge amount of work, companies that have planned carefully for success in the transformation process normally make enormous profits.

This book will help to make the rather complex IPO process easier to understand by breaking it down into steps. It can also help the reader decide if going public is the best next step for the company or if there are other procedures the company should do first to better ready itself for an IPO. If, after reading this book, the business owner feels the company is not ready to go public, I offer some ways the business owner can make the company ready to go public through transition alternatives.

From 1990 to 2002, there was on average at least one IPO in the United States every day. The exact number of IPOs varied from year to year, with some years seeing fewer than 100 and others more than 400 offerings. Approximately $490 billion was raised through these IPOs, an average of $80 million per offering. At the end of the first day of trading, an IPO company's shares traded on average 18.8 percent above the price at which the company sold the shares. Yet despite this trend many companies failed to achieve results they hoped for during the first three years after going public, significantly underperforming the market in both share price and profits.

This not-so-good news about IPOs was for a long time not well known. The financial press would rather cover highly successful companies, including such legendary performers as Yahoo!, Microsoft, and Amazon.com. The IPO downside finally came to the forefront of the news with the fall of the numerous Internet service providers who declared bankruptcy or simply disappeared. The contrast between the winners and the losers has inspired me to undertake this book and to analyze what happened in order to help business owners manage the IPO transformation process successfully. My unique approach is to identify steps to a successful IPO by implementing the "Balanced Scorecard" approach.

THE BALANCED SCORECARD

The Balanced Scorecard approach is the synthesis between the irresistible force to build long-range competitive capabilities and the immovable object of the historical-cost financial accounting model.

The Balanced Scorecard retains traditional financial measures, but financial measures only tell the story of past events, which was all that was needed for Industrial Age companies. But for guiding and evaluating the journey that Information Age companies must make to create value through investment in customers, suppliers, employees, processes, technology, and innovation, such financial measures are inadequate.

In the Balanced Scorecard, financial measures of past performance are complemented with measures of the drivers of future performance. An organization's vision and strategy are incorporated into the objectives and measures of the scorecard, taking four distinct perspectives (1) finances, (2) customers, (3) internal business processes, and (4) learning and growth. These provide the framework for the Balanced Scorecard.

The Balanced Scorecard expands business unit objectives beyond summary financial measures. A company's management team can now measure how their businesses create value for both future and current customers and how they must enhance internal capabilities and the investment in systems, procedures, and people necessary to improve future performance. The Balanced Scorecard captures the critical value-creation activities undertaken by motivated and skilled organizational participants. It reveals the value drivers for superior long-term financial and competitive performance while retaining, through the financial perspective, an interest in short-term performance.

THE IPO AS A TRANSFORMATION PROCESS

This book will examine the IPO more broadly than it is usually considered. It will look at the IPO not as an end in itself, but as a milestone in a larger process. My goal is to help the company's management team ascertain whether it is in the company's best interest to become a public company or to remain private for the time being. Timing is everything in the IPO process. I also want to make clear the roles of the various participants in the IPO process, among them the Securities and Exchange Commission (SEC), the financial community, and a variety of stakeholders. In describing the IPO process itself, I also discuss how to work with underwriters, auditors, and other advisors.

Many companies already have performance measurement systems that incorporate nonfinancial as well as financial measures, so what's new about a proposal for a "balanced" set of measures? While virtually all organizations do indeed have both types, many use their nonfinancial measures merely for local improvements, at front-line and customer-contact operations. Senior managers meanwhile use aggregate financial measures as if these measures summarize adequately the results of all the operations performed by mid- and lower-level employees. These organizations are using their performance measures, financial and nonfinancial, only for control of short-term operations and tactical feedback.

The Balanced Scorecard emphasizes that both financial and nonfinancial measures must be part of the information system for employees at all levels of the organization. Front-line employees must understand the financial consequences of their decisions and actions. Senior executives must understand the drivers of long-term financial success.

The objectives and the measures for the Balanced Scorecard, on the other hand, are more than just an ad hoc collection of performance measures. They are derived from a top-down process driven by the strategy and mission of the organizational unit. The Balanced Scorecard should translate the business unit's strategy and mission into tangible objectives and measures that balance external measures for customers and shareholders and internal measures of critical business innovation, processes, and learning and growth. The measures balance outcome measures, the results from past efforts, and input measures that drive future performance. The scorecard is also balanced between objective, easily quantified outcome measures, and subjective performance drivers.

SHORT- AND LONG-TERM PERSPECTIVES

Research clearly shows that highly successful companies tend to treat their IPOs as a process. Those that were unsuccessful often treated theirs as simply a financing transaction. That is why we will discuss in detail the elements that are conducive to outstanding performance, from both the short-term perspective of the market and the long-term perspective of the company.

Those who consider the IPO as just a short-term financial transaction, underestimate its far-reaching impact. An IPO can mark a turning point in the life of a company. With this one event, the company can accelerate its growth, launch new products, enter new markets, and attract valuable employees. The IPO is part of a valuation process, a process of transformation from a successful private company to successful public company. As a public company, it must continually deliver value to its stakeholders (shareholders, customers, employees, vendors, etc.). The IPO event itself is only one component of this process. The IPO generally lasts only 90 to 120 days. The valuation process begins at least a year or two before the IPO and continues well beyond it.

MANAGEMENT'S ROLE

It is up to management to anticipate the challenges that will arise throughout the valuation process and lead the company past the major transactional milestones. An IPO places management, usually the CEO, in an odd position. He is called on to be the quarterback in a game he has never played, which will call upon all the leadership qualities he can muster. CEOs guiding companies through IPOs have to be visionary and architect, quarterback and cheerleader, spokesperson and manager.

Above all, CEOs and those who report directly to them must become evangelists whose fervent vision can motivate a variety of stakeholders and move the company to a competitive advantage. Much of the success of an IPO depends on the credibility and trust that management can build, the employees' trust that the management will lead them in a beneficial direction and the market's trust that management will deliver on its strategic plan.

The IPO process is filled with land mines. Why do some companies succeed dramatically while others fail? What critical factors set the managers of highly successful IPO companies apart from their peers?

Highly successful companies are those that have outperformed the competition before as well as during and after the IPO. Competitive position at the time of the offering is particularly critical. The stronger the firm was before the IPO, the more successful it tended to be after. Conversely, the risks of going public were higher for those that were less competitive at the start.

The highly successful companies were significantly stronger than their public competitors according to all criteria, financial and nonfinancial (Kaplan, 1997). As a result, highly successful companies went public with share prices that averaged 20 percent higher than those of unsuccessful companies. At the time of their IPOs, highly successful companies had an average market value that was $59 million greater than the market value of unsuccessful companies. Three years later, the gap had widened to more than $200 million. The average value of highly successful companies doubled during the first three years after the IPO, while unsuccessful companies lost an average of 10 percent of their value during the same period.

Highly successful companies began to transform themselves into public companies months or years in advance of the IPO. These companies viewed the IPO as part of a process rather than as an isolated event. Recognizing this, they introduced new approaches or system enhancements, executed strategic transactions, and implemented strong communication programs. The most successful companies made improvements in their employee incentive programs (Baron, 1999). These changes were believed to have had a greater impact on the company's subsequent performance than any of the other 17 policies and practices that were cited. Highly successful companies also tended to be distinguished by improvements in strategic planning, internal controls, financial accounting and reporting, executive compensation, and investor relations policies.

It is especially important to note that the earlier the change initiatives were put in place, the more likely was the success of the IPO. Those that launched such programs a year or more before the IPO were much more likely to achieve success.

Nonfinancial factors are critical. The most successful companies ranked high on such nonfinancial measures as credibility and quality of management, retention of employees, customer service, and strength of the corporate culture. They tended to be ahead of competitors in building a winning team, installing an information-based infrastructure, and drawing on the advice of experienced and objective business advisors. These efforts won them the attention of the most successful venture capitalists and underwriters, which further supported their higher offering prices and brought them a stronger reception from investors.

UNDERSTANDING THE C CORPORATION

The decision to launch an IPO often means a decision to change the structure of the business. Table 2-1 compares the most common forms of business entities, sole proprietor, partnership, S corporation, C corporation, and limited liability company. Each entity has unique legal and tax characteristics. Once the decision is made to sell stock to the public, the business must adopt the C corporation structure. Whether that is the best choice requires careful consideration.

MAKING THE COMMITMENT

While there are many areas of concern in selecting the proper form for a business and in deciding whether to change the form, at the forefront are issues of the formalities required to bring the company into existence, regulatory compliance, management and control, personal liability, and tax treatment. These will differ for each venture. However, in choosing to make an IPO, managers are making a definite commitment to the C corporation, so it is important to understand what that involves.

The C corporation, which is what most people are thinking of when they use the word "corporation," is probably the best-understood form of business entity, perhaps because it is by definition public. The form is permitted by law in every state. It is separate and distinct from its

TABLE 2-1
BUSINESS STRUCTURES COMPARED

	Sole Proprietorship	Partnership	S Corporation	C Corporation	Limited Liability Company
Formation	No formal document required	No formal document required.	Yes, a formal filing is required.	Yes, a formal filing is required.	Yes, a formal filing is required
States that permit the formation	All	All	All	All	48 (except Hawaii and Vermont)
Form to be filed with federal tax returns	Form 1040	Form 1065	Form 1120S	Form 1120	Form 1065 or Form 1120, depending on charter.
Formation document	None	Partnership Agreement	Articles or Certificates of	Articles or Certificates of Incorporation	Articles of Organization Incorporation
Limitation on number of owners	Yes (restricted to one).	No (must have at least two).	Yes (cannot have more than 75).	No	No
Limited liability protection	No	No	Yes	No	No
Limitation on having owners that are partnerships, corporations, or non-resident aliens.	No	No	Yes	Yes	Yes
Life of the entity	Same as owner	Same as owners	Unlimited	Unlimited	Same as owners
Free transferability of ownership	Yes	No	Yes	Yes	No
Ability to raise capital	Low	Moderate	Very good	Very good	Moderate

TABLE 2-1 (CONT.)
BUSINESS STRUCTURES COMPARED

	Sole Proprietorship	Partnership	S Corporation	C Corporation	Limited Liability Company
Management control or structure	Centralized control	Decentralized control (all partners direct participants in management).	Centralized control	Centralized control	Centralized control
Basis for treatment of ownership interest	Cash contributed + basis of property contributed.	Cash contributed +basis of property contributed + any gain recognized + increased share of partnership liabilities.	Cash contributed + basis of property contributed + any gain recognized.	Cash contributed + basis of property contributed + any gain recognized.	Same as partnership.
Accounting period— taxable year	Same tax year as owner.	Restricted to: 1. Majority ñ interest tax year. 2. Principal partnerís tax year. 3. Least aggregate deferral of partners' income or • Make a section 444 election, or • Establish a business purpose for using a different taxable year.	Generally uses a calendar year or 1. Make a section 444 election. 2. Establish a business purposefor using a different taxable year.	No restriction.	Same as partnership.
Permissible accounting method	Same method as the owner.	No restriction. Cash method is prohibited if the partnership has: 1. At least one corporation partner or 2. It is a tax shelter.	No restriction	Accrual method, unless it is PSC, farming, or has gross income less than $5 million.	Same as partnership.
"Pass through" entity	Yes	Yes	Yes	No	Yes

TABLE 2-1 (CONT.)
BUSINESS STRUCTURES COMPARED

	Sole Proprietorship	Partnership	S Corporation	C Corporation	Limited Liability Company
Entity-level federal tax (assuming in LLC is structured to be taxed as a partnership).	No	No	No	No	No
Double taxation of income	No	No	No	Yes	No
Limitation on losses	Allowed to carry back losses 2 years and carry-forward 20 years.	Allowed to pass through loss to partners for deduction, which is limited to: 1. Partner's basis. 2. At-risk level. 3. Passive activity rules.	Same as partnership.	Two-year loss carry-back; 20-year carry-forward (Loss cannot be passed through to shareholders for deduction.)	Same as partnership.
Fringe benefits deductible	No	No, except for: 1. Accident and health-care plans. 2. Meals and lodging for the convenience of the employer. 3. Group term life insurance. 4. Cafeteria plans.	No, unless a shareholder owns less than 2% of the stock.	Yes	Same as partnership.
Fringe benefits taxable to employees	Yes	Yes	Yes	No	Yes
Social Security (self-employment) tax	Yes. Amount paid is equal to the sum of employee and employer payments.	Yes. Paid on both wages and partnership income when received.	Yes. Paid on wages when received. Income flowing through to shareholders is not subject to SS tax.	Yes. Corporation matches employee payment but is allowed to deduct the amount paid.	Yes. Members are subject to tax.

owners or shareholders. As a separate entity, a corporation, not the shareholders, is liable for its debts and other obligations. A corporation may acquire, hold, and dispose of property, and conduct business, and sue or be sued in its own name. Once a corporation is formed it must hold shareholder meetings and record the minutes of every meeting. Generally, the relative rights and duties of the corporation, its management, and its owners are defined by statutes and by the corporation bylaws and certificate of incorporation.

For federal tax purposes, certain business entities are automatically classified as corporations and taxed that way. However, in 1997, the rules on businesses taxed as a corporation were changed for businesses formed after 1996. The rules will be discussed in detail later in the "Formation and Filing Requirement" section.

GENERAL CHARACTERISTICS

Unlike a sole proprietorship or an S corporation, there is no restriction on the number of owners or stockholders (shareholders) a C corporation can have, and it has many more opportunities to raise additional capital, not the least of which is the IPO. Moreover, shareholders are free to sell their shares and the business continues irrespective of the lives of the shareholders, definite non-tax advantages over other business forms. A corporation carries on indefinitely until it is dissolved by a vote of the shareholders, which means that for all practical purposes, the corporation has unlimited life. Another distinguishing feature is that the liability of corporation shareholders is limited. In a properly organized and maintained corporation, shareholders have no personal liability for the debts of the corporation, they are liable only to the extent of their equity investment in the corporation. If the corporation does not have enough assets to satisfy its liabilities, creditors may not seek satisfaction or financial recourse from the personal assets of shareholders. In businesses operated as sole proprietorships or partnerships, owners have unlimited liability for debts incurred in the business.

MANAGEMENT CONTROL

Management in a C corporation is centralized. It generally rests on the board of directors who are elected by the shareholders. Unlike what happens in a sole proprietorship, general partnership, or limited liability corporation, the shareholders in a C corporation do not have the right to direct participation in management. Aside from the right to elect directors and approve certain transactions, such as mergers, sale of all assets, and dissolution, shareholders have no role in managing the corporation. However, if a business is a "close corporation" (one with a specified maximum number of stockholders) management may be vested in the shareholders, who are also the members of the board of directors.

FORMATION AND FILING REQUIREMENTS

Since 1997 when the tax rule has been changed, if the following types of business were formed after 1996, they can be considered corporations and taxed as such:

- A business entity wholly owned by a state or local government.
- A corporation formed under a federal or state law.
- A business formed under a state law that refers to the business as a joint-stock company or joint-stock association.
- An insurance company.
- Certain foreign businesses.
- A state-chartered business entity conducting banking activities.
- Certain publicly traded partnerships that specifically are required to be taxed as a corporation by the Internal Revenue Code.

Any business formed before 1997 that was taxed as a corporation under old rules will continue to be taxed as a corporation. An eligible entity that chooses not to be classified as a corporation can file Form 8832 to get approval from the IRS to elect another classification.

FILING REQUIREMENTS

Corporations must file an income tax return every year whether or not they have taxable income for that year. Most corporations usually figure their income tax liability and report the income, deductions, gains and losses by using Form 1120, the corporation tax return, but corporations can use the Form 1120A, the corporation short-form return, if they meet certain requirements:

- All the corporation's gross receipts, total income, and total assets are less than $500,000.
- The corporation has no foreign shareholders that directly or indirectly own 25 percent or more of its stock.
- The corporation's only dividend income is from domestic corporations, and it qualifies for the 70 percent deduction.
- The corporation is not:
  — A personal holding company.
  — A member of a controlled group.
  — Filing a consolidated return.
  — Dissolving or liquidating.
  — Required to file one of the returns listed under Special Returns for Certain Organizations.

Generally, a corporation must file its return by the 15th day of the third month after the end of its tax year. A dissolved corporation must file by the 15th day of the third month after the date of dissolution. If it has found an error in a previously filed return the corporation can use Form 1120X to amend its previous filing. Corporations can also request extensions of the usual deadlines by using Form 7004, which gives them another six months to file the income tax return. A corporation that does not file its return on time, including extensions, may be penalized from 5 to 25 percent of the unpaid tax unless it has provided a reasonable statement explaining the delay.

Tax Characteristics

Business owners can use the corporation structure to retain more after-tax profits to grow and expand the business. Of all the major business entity forms, the corporation is the only one that pays tax at the business level on the taxable income. Unlike the general partnership, where the partners are not considered apart from the entity, a corporation and its shareholders are considered as separate entities. Therefore, corporate income is taxed on the corporation instead of the shareholder level.

The corporation is liable for its own taxable income, its profits. When the corporation distributes the profits to its shareholders as dividends, the shareholders will be taxed when they receive those dividends. This is the double taxation problem, which will be discussed later.

Moreover, although the profits of the corporation can be (but need not be) distributed as dividend to its shareholders, unlike with the S corporation, corporate losses cannot be passed on to shareholders, who cannot deduct any losses of the corporation on their individual tax returns.

No gain or loss is recognized if property is contributed to a corporation (1) by one or more persons solely in exchange for stock in the corporation, and (2) such persons are immediately in control of the corporation after the exchange. Shareholders must own at least 80 percent of the stock in order to control the corporation. In other words, a person who after making a contribution in return for stock owns more than 80 percent of the corporation's stock is considered as immediately controlling the corporate stock.

Generally, this non-recognition rule in the contribution applied on a corporation is more restrictive than on a partnership or a sole proprietorship, because the shareholders that contribute property to the Corporation must immediately control the corporation after the contribution.

BASIS IN FORMATION OF A CORPORATION

When a shareholder contributes property in exchange for an ownership interest, two assets are created. The shareholder has a basis in the stock and the business entity will have a basis in the property it receives. Typically, the basis rules for a C corporation and an S corporation are the same. When a shareholder contributes property in exchange for the corporate stock, the shareholder's basis in the stock is the same as the basis of the property contributed to the corporation. The corporation in its turn has the same basis the shareholder had in the property.

ACCOUNTING

The accounting methodology among C corporations is quite complex in the level of sophistication required to prepare financial forms versus those of any other entity types. The C corporation's owners are its shareholders as opposed to an individual or partners, and therefore require much more due diligence on the part of the accounting staff than those of non-publicly held corporations, partnerships, etc.

TAXABLE YEAR

A new corporation establishes its tax year when it files its first tax return. Unlike other business entities, corporations can choose any accounting period (a calendar year or a fiscal year ending in any month) as their taxable year. Once a choice is made, if a corporation wishes to change to a different accounting period it must usually file an application, Form 1128, with the IRS to get an approval for the change. However, if it meets all the following requirements, the corporation can change its tax year without IRS approval:

- It has not changed its accounting period during the 10 calendar years ending with the calendar year that includes the beginning of the short tax period required to effect the change. (The short tax period begins on the first day after the end of the corporation's previous tax year and ends the day before the first day of its new tax year.)
- The short tax period cannot be a taxable year in which the corporation has a net operating loss.
- The corporation's taxable income for the short tax year must be at least 80 percent of its taxable income for the previous tax year.
- It cannot apply to become an S corporation for the tax year that would follow the short tax period required to effect the change.

ACCOUNTING METHODOLOGY

A corporation must use the accrual method of accounting if its average annual gross receipts exceed $5 million. It is not allowed to use the cash method of accounting because that would make it too easy for it to manipulate its cash receipts and disbursement transactions to get a tax advantage. However, a corporation can be exempted from this restriction if it is a (1) farming business, (2) qualified personal service corporation, and (3) corporation with gross receipts of not more than $5 million. Generally, if average annual gross receipts for the three immediately previous taxable years do not exceed $5 million, the corporation can use the cash method of accounting.

Like a partnership or S corporation, the C corporation is allowed to change the accounting method it currently uses to report taxable income by filing Form 3115, Application for Change in Accounting Method, with the IRS. Without IRS approval, any change in accounting method will not be taken into account.

THE DOUBLE TAXATION PROBLEM

A C corporation may pay salaries to its shareholders for services rendered and distribute cash to shareholders in the form of dividends. The corporation may deduct the salary payment but not the dividend, so dividend payouts are still considered part of taxable corporation income. The dividends are taxed as shareholder income when they are received. This system, usually referred to as double taxation, is one of the main disadvantages of a C corporation.

ALLOCATION OF OPERATING INCOME AND LOSS

If the deductions of a C corporation for the year are more than the income for the year, the corporation will have a net operating loss (NOL). Though losses from an S corporation can flow through to the shareholders and may be used to offset shareholders' other income, that is not true for shareholders in a C corporation, so a C corporation cannot distribute its net operating loss to its shareholders.

Although the losses cannot pass to shareholders for deduction, the C Corporation can deduct an NOL from corporate income in other years. It can carry back its losses to reduce taxable income in previous years and then carry forward any remaining losses to reduce income in future years. Since 1997, the carry-back period has been two years and the carry-forward period has been 20 years.

A C corporation may choose not to carry back its losses but to use the NOL only in the future. To do this, the corporation must attach to its tax return for the NOL year a statement that it chooses to forgo the carry-back period.

ALTERNATIVE MINIMUM TAX

A C corporation, like an individual, is subject to the alternative minimum tax (AMT). The purpose of the corporate AMT is to ensure that corporations pay at least some tax on their income. Generally, the corporation needs to make adjustments of regular tax items to obtain its alternative minimum taxable income (AMTI). The amount of the AMT is then computed by applying the appropriate tax rate to the AMTI. Typically, a corporation needs to pay the AMT if its tentative AMT is greater than its regular tax, and the regular tax if the AMT is less. The following examples show how the AMT can effect a corporation.

Example 1. If Jones Corporation has a tentative AMT of $50,000 and its regular tax liability is $30,000 for the current year, what will happen?

- Since its tentative AMT, $50,000, is more than its regular tax liability, $30,000. Jones Corporation is subject to AMT and must pay the $50,000 tax.
- Within the $50,000, the corporation is considered to be making a payment of $30,000 in regular tax liability and $20,000 in AMT ($50,000 ñ 30,000 = 20,000).

Example 2. If Jones Corporation's regular tax liability is $60,000, which is more than its tentative AMT of $50,000, the corporation must pay $60,000 in regular tax liability and is not subject to any AMT.

Furthermore, since 1997, a small corporation will not owe any AMT if it meets any of the following requirements:

- It is the corporation's first tax year.
- It is the corporation's second tax year and gross income for the first tax year was less than $5 million.
- It is the third tax year and average gross income for the previous two years was less than $5 million.
- It is the fourth tax year and average gross income for the first three years was less than $5 million.
- It is the fifth tax year and average gross income for (1) its first three years was less than $5 million and (2) all later three-year periods and ending before the current tax year was less than $7.5 million.

ACCUMULATED EARNINGS TAX

Of all types of businesses, only the C corporation is subject to the accumulated earnings tax. The purpose of the accumulated earnings tax is to prevent the C corporation from accumulating earnings beyond its reasonable needs. The accumulated earnings tax is thus a penalty tax. The C corporation is generally allowed to accumulate $250,000 or more of its earnings for possible expansion or other business needs. If the corporation has unreasonable accumulated earnings, it will be subject to accumulated earnings tax at a rate of 39.6 percent. (The allowable accumulation is $150,000 for a business whose principal function is performing services in (1) law, (2) accounting, (3) architecture, (4) health, or (5) consulting.)

Although the accumulated earnings tax applies to almost every corporation, there are still some exceptions. The tax does not apply to a personal holding company, domestic or foreign, or to a corporation exempt from tax under subchapter F.

FRINGE BENEFITS

When a C corporation provides fringe benefits to employees, the best deal is when the corporation can deduct the cost of the fringe benefits and the employees do not have to include the value of the benefit in their taxable income. Typically, the cost of benefits is considered an ordinary and necessary business expense and is therefore deductible by the corporation.

The favorable treatment of fringe benefits can be an important reason for using a C corporation to conduct a business. Unlike other entities, a C corporation is allowed to deduct shareholder payments made in the form of wages (salaries) for services rendered and fringe benefits because the entity and its shareholders are treated as separate taxpaying entities and shareholders can be employees of the corporation. Fringe benefits for owner-employees can also help the entity to reduce its total tax liability. Eight examples of these fringe benefits are:

1. Payment of premiums for health insurance.
2. The cost of providing up to $50,000 of group term life insurance.
3. Payment for injuries or sickness directly paid by the employer.

4. Meals or lodging furnished for the convenience of the employer.

5. Cafeteria plans.

6. De minimis fringe benefits, award programs, gifts, meal money.

7. Educational assistance programs.

8. Dependent care assistance programs.

SOCIAL SECURITY TAX

The Social Security tax is based on salaries or wages. The employer is generally liable for the employer share of the tax. In other words, C corporations are required to match employee payments into the Social Security system. The maximum amount of wages subject to Social Security tax changes from time to time. Generally, the Corporation can deduct the amount it paid in Social Security taxes when calculating its taxable income.

CORPORATE DISTRIBUTION

A corporation can make a distribution to its shareholders in the form of money, stock, or other property. Any distributions to the shareholders from either current or accumulated earnings or profits are generally considered a dividend. When a C corporation distributes the dividend to its shareholders, the shareholders must include the dividend received in their gross income.

If the corporation distributes property to shareholders, they must recognize income equal to the fair market value of the property in their gross income. On the other hand, the corporations does not have to recognize any gain or loss on the distribution of the property unless the fair market value of the property exceeds its adjusted basis, in which case the corporation should recognize a gain. There are no exceptions for losses.

SUMMARY

This chapter provided an overview of the C corporation, discussing factors that should be considered in deciding whether to commit to a C corporation by issuing an IPO. The C corporation has several advantages over alternative business structures, such as non-taxable owner-employee fringe benefits, multiple classes of stocks, continuity of life of the enterprise, and no restriction on the number and type of shareholders. A major advantage is that shareholders are for the most part protected from personal liability for any activity by the corporation. Liability for corporate debts is limited to the corporation unless shareholders have signed personal guarantees.

A C corporation does have some significant disadvantages. One is the double taxation system in which the profits are taxed at the corporation level and then when distributed as dividends are taxed again to the shareholder. In addition, unlike an S corporation, a C corporation cannot distribute operating losses to shareholders for deduction. Entrepreneurs who expect to have significant losses in the early years may want to postpone using this structure to conduct their business in the early stages.

IS AN IPO THE RIGHT STRATEGY?

Going public is not for every company. The pitfalls are numerous and the stakes are high, much like a game of poker! Poor timing or inadequate planning and preparation can jeopardize an IPO. The fairy-tale success stories we've all heard are counterbalanced by many tales of plunging share prices, litigation, management shakeout, and loss of management control. Some of the unsuccessful public companies would have failed even as private companies, but others could have avoided disaster by canceling their IPOs or just postponing them.

The rigors and the magnitude of managing a public company, even a successful one, intimidate many company management teams. It must be ascertained if an IPO is really the best strategy the company. In deciding whether going public is the right thing to do, managers must weigh the benefits against and drawbacks.

BENEFITS AND OPPORTUNITIES

The benefits of going public are numerous and diverse. To determine whether they outweigh the drawbacks, it's important to use the perspective of the Balanced Scorecard, in the context of corporate, shareholder, and personal objectives. The most appealing benefits and opportunities are these:

- **Enhanced financial condition.** Selling shares to the public, which brings money that does not have to be repaid, enhances a company's financial condition immediately.

- **Increase in shareholder value.** Starting from the initial offering, the value of the stock may increase tremendously. Shares that are publicly traded generally command higher prices than those do that are not. There are at least three reasons why investors are usually willing to pay more for public companies (1) the shares are easily marketable, (2) public companies are assumed to be more mature and sophisticated, and (3) information about the company is more readily available.

- **Diversification of current shareholder portfolios.** Those who already own shares in the company before the IPO are now able to diversify their investment portfolios. IPOs often include a secondary offering of shares already owned by investors in the company in addition to the primary offering of new shares. Potential investors, however, must not perceive that the secondary offering means existing shareholders are abandoning the stock. For that reason, underwriters will normally restrict the number of shares that can be sold in a secondary offering.

- **Additional capital to perpetuate growth.** The net proceeds from the sale of shares in a public offering provide additional working capital for the company, a clear benefit. The company can use the capital for general corporate purposes or for specific projects. It might use the capital to acquire other businesses, to finance research and development, to repay debt, and to acquire or modernize production facilities.

- **Higher market value for the company.** Raising equity capital through a public offering often results in a higher valuation for the company through a higher multiple of earnings (earnings ratio), as compared with other types of private financing, which will be discussed later. Therefore, it often results in less dilution of ownership than with some other financing alternatives, such as venture capital. Raising capital in an IPO also avoids the interest costs and cash drain of debt financing.

• *Improved opportunities for future financing.* By going public, a company usually improves its net worth and builds a broader equity base. The improved debt-to-equity ratio can help the company reduce its current cost of borrowing or make it easier to borrow additional funds as needed. If the stock performs well in the aftermarket, the company will also be able to raise additional equity capital on favorable terms. Once there is an established market for its stock, the company has the flexibility to offer future investors a whole new range of securities with liquidity and an ascertainable market value.

• *Greater potential for mergers and acquisitions.* Well-conceived acquisitions can play a big part in corporate success as well as survival, but private companies often lack the financial connections and resources to take an aggressive role in mergers and acquisitions. A merger can be the path to instant product diversification and quick completion of product lines. It also can bring greater executive depth, advanced technical knowledge, economies of scale, improved access to financing, entry into otherwise closed markets, vertical or horizontal integration of operations, and new marketing strength. Going public enhances a company's financing alternatives for acquisitions by adding two vital components to its financial resources (1) additional money derived from the IPO and (2) unissued equity shares that are readily marketable.

Public companies often issue stock, rather than paying cash, to acquire other businesses. The owners of an acquisition target may be more willing to accept stock that is publicly traded. The liquidity provided by the public market gives the company being acquired greater flexibility to sell shares as best suits its interest, or use the shares as collateral for loans.

The public market can also make it easier to value company shares. If shares are privately held, a stakeholder may have to estimate the value and hope the owners of the other company will agree. If they do not, the stakeholder will have to negotiate to get a fair price. When shares are publicly traded, the price per share generally is set every day in the stock market.

- *Enhanced corporate image and increased employee motivation.* Indirect strengthening of its competitive position by having a public market for its securities can enhance the company's corporate image. The attention of the press and financial community at large is focused on the company as it goes public. Therefore, the company receives free publicity and word-of-mouth advertising. In addition, some of the company's customers and suppliers may buy shares in the IPO, which may lead to new loyalties and enhanced relationships.

  Once a public market for its shares has been established, the company is better able to attract and retain key employees by offering them stock options, stock purchase plans, and stock appreciation rights. These popular compensation arrangements not only conserve cash and offer tax advantages but also increase employee motivation and loyalty.

- *Stock exchange listing.* A goal of many companies that go public is simply to be listed on a stock exchange. A listing facilitates trading in the company's stock and fosters public recognition because the financial press tends to watch listed companies more closely.

DRAWBACKS

The potential benefits must be weighed against the drawbacks and obligations of going public, in the context of the company's overall and shareholder objectives. In many cases, by thinking ahead a company can minimize the impact of these drawbacks through careful planning and enlisting the expertise of outside professional advisors. The most significant drawbacks are these:

- *Loss of company control.* Depending on the proportion of shares sold to the public, the previously private stakeholders may be at risk of losing control of the public company, now or in the future. Retaining at least 51 percent of the shares will help ensure control at first, but subsequent offerings and acquisitions may dilute that control. Wide distribution of the company's shares will ensure that there is no concentration of voting power in a few hands, reducing the immediate threat to control

of the company, but the company may nevertheless be suscepti-
ble to a hostile or unfriendly takeover.

However, if the stock is widely distributed, management usually can retain control even if it retains less than 50 percent of
the shares. The company can also retain voting control by issuing a new class of common stock with limited voting rights.
However, this class of stock may also met limited demand by
investors and therefore may sell for less than ordinary common
stock.

- *Sharing the company's success.* By contributing their capital,
  investors share the risk of the business—but they also will share
  the company's success. Management must ask, however,
  whether their share of the business success would be dispropor-
  tionate. A company that realistically anticipates unusually high
  earnings in the next two to three years, and can obtain bank or
  other financing, may wish to defer its IPO. Then, when the
  company does go public, the shares will command a higher
  price. Again, the overall success of the company must be balanced against the perceived prestige that comes from operating
  a public company.

- *Loss of control over information.* Of all the changes that occur
  when a company goes public, perhaps none can be more prob-
  lematic than the loss of privacy. When the company goes public,
  the Securities and Exchange Commission (SEC) requires it to
  disclose much information that private companies do not ordinarily disclose. Some of these disclosures may be highly sensitive —compensation paid to key executives and directors, special incentives for management, and plans and strategies that
  under-gird the company's operations. Although these disclosures
  need not cover every detail of a company's operations, all information that could significantly affect investors' decisions must
  be disclosed. Although difficult, however, these disclosures
  rarely harm the company. For the most part, market forces gov-
  ern employee compensation and the prices the company pays for
  materials and receives for its products–not the disclosed financial results.

Recognizing the loss of privacy an IPO brings, though, some companies feel that they should discontinue special arrangements with key personnel or related parties that might be normal for private companies but misconstrued by outsiders. An example would be the lease of assets from an entity that is wholly owned by a director.

- *A limit of management's freedom to act.* In going public, management agrees to surrender some degree of freedom. Whereas managers of a privately held company generally are free to act as they deem reasonable, managers of a public company must obtain the approval of the board of directors on certain major matters. On specified matters, they must even seek the consent of the shareholders.

  Obtaining directors' approval need not be a significant problem. The board of directors, if kept well informed, can usually be counted on to understand management's needs, offer support, and grant much of the desired flexibility.

- *Extensive periodic reporting and accountability.* As a public company, the company will be subject to the reporting requirements of the SEC–quarterly financial reporting (Form 10-Q), annual financial reporting (Form 10-K), prompt reporting of current material events (Form 8-K), and various other requirements such as reporting sales of control shares (shares held by controlling shareholders) and tender offers. These requirements, which include the fact that financial statements must be audited, usually means that financial and other information must be more extensive and timely. This may create a need for improved accounting information systems, more (or more sophisticated) accounting staff, and more consultation with lawyers, auditors, and other outside advisors. Securities analysts and the financial press will add their demands on the company and its executives. In summary, costs of doing business will increase.

- *Initial and continuing expense.* Going public can be costly and will call for a tremendous commitment of management's time and energy. The largest single cost in an IPO is ordinarily the underwriter's discount or commission, which generally ranges from 6 to 10 percent of the offering price. In addition, legal and accounting fees, printing costs, the underwriter's out-of-pocket expenses (generally not included in the commission), filing fees, and registrar and transfer agent fees can typically add another $300,000 to $600,000 (Beatty and Welch, 1996). The exact costs depend on such factors as the complexity of the registration statement, the extent to which legal counsel must be involved, management's familiarity with the reporting requirements for a public company, and the availability of recent audited financial statements. These expenses generally are not deductible for income tax purposes. On the other hand, they also do not affect the company's reported net income, because under generally accepted accounting principles (GAAP), they are treated as part of a capital transaction and thus deducted from the proceeds of the offering.

Beyond the initial offering, there are the continuing costs of the reports and proxy statements that must be filed periodically with regulatory agencies and distributed to shareholders and the increased professional fees for lawyers, accountants, registrars, and transfer agents. The time managers will spend preparing these reports and statements must be taken into account as well, because this responsibility will divert their attention from daily operations.

The company may also need to upgrade its information systems to enable it to maintain adequate financial records and systems of internal controls to meet the accounting provision of the Foreign Corrupt Practices Act, which is part of the Securities Exchange Act of 1934. Upgraded systems also may be necessary to keep financial information timely.

• **_Limits on major shareholders._** Controlling or major shareholders of a public company are not free to sell their shares at will. The SEC has restrictions on when and how many shares insiders may sell. The company must be aware of these restrictions when it plans an IPO. Additionally, under penalty of criminal as well as civil, no one may take advantage of inside information before it becomes public. Another restriction applies to short-swing profits. In certain cases insiders who realize a gain on a company's stock within six months of its purchase must return that gain to the company whether or not the trading was based on inside information.

- *New fiduciary responsibilities*. When a business is private, the money the company invests or puts at risk was the company's own liability. Once the company is public, the money and risk now belong to the shareholders, to whom the company is now accountable. Therefore, the company must approach potential conflicts of interest with the utmost caution. Additionally, it will be necessary to work with the board of directors to help them discharge their fiduciary responsibilities on corporate matters.

CHAPTER 4

IPO AFTERMARKET RETURNS

There has been considerable research into the performance of IPOs. A study of 1,526 IPOs from 1984–1995 performed by Charles J. Kaplan (1997) found that from opening to close of the first trading day, IPOs produced an average return of 16.4 percent. Kaplan also found that for the three years after the IPO, for over 80 percent of the stocks, the valuation underperformed market expectations. He concludes, in fact, that on average an investor would have been ended up with only 83 cents compared to a dollar invested in the similar non IPO firms.

Kaplan has two explanations for the generally poor long-term performance of IPOs. First, periodically investors are overly optimistic about the future earnings growth of new, emerging companies. Second, firms take advantage of these overly optimistic periods by choosing to go public at these times. IPO activity late in the 1990s surely demonstrates both.

Even before Kaplan's study, Jay R. Ritter (1995) had found that on average IPOs generally underperform similar non-IPO companies over a period of three years. He also found that investing in IPOs over the five years before his study would have resulted in a return of $0.83 compared to each dollar of return in a similar non-IPO company.

Tim Loughran and Jay R. Ritter (1997) looked into the long-run performance of IPO companies and seasoned equity offerings (SEOs) companies. (SEOs are secondary or post-secondary offerings of equity shares.) They compared the long-term performance of 4,753 companies that issued stock between 1975 and 1995 and of similar-sized companies that did not issue stock during the study period. The researchers found that investors in the IPO companies studied would have had average annual returns of only 5 percent and investors in the SEO companies would have received an average annual return of only 7 percent.

Meanwhile, companies similar to the IPO and SEO firms that did not issue stock had average annual returns of 12 percent and 15 percent, respectively. Loughran and Ritter find that besides being poor performers, the IPO and SEO firms carry more risk than do the non-stock-issuing companies studied. They hypothesize that stock-issuing firms take advantage of times when stocks in general are overvalued in order to get investors to pay more for their stock.

The findings of Ritter (1995) and Loughran and Ritter (1997) provide important information on the long-term underperformance of IPOs, information that should inform the decision of any company considering an IPO. The authors also examine how initial day underpricing affects the long-run performance of IPO firms.

THE ROOTS OF IPO PERFORMANCE

In studying the long-run underperformance of IPOs, Alon Brav and Paul A. Gompers (1997) particularly compared companies backed by venture capital with those that were not. They looked at IPO and non-IPO firms between 1980 and 1992. In contrast with Ritter (1995), Brav and Gompers found that when IPO firms were matched with similar non-IPO firms, the IPOs did not underperform. The measurement period for this study was the opening price on the second day of IPO trading to the closing price five years later. The sample looked at 934 venture-backed IPOs and 3,407 other IPOs issued between 1980 and 1992.

Brav and Gompers are convinced that underperformance is a smaller-company phenomenon. In their opinion, small, low-book-to-market value firms will underperform larger firms whether or not the smaller firms are IPOs. They also use the mid-1980s recession to explain the underperformance of small companies, who had trouble raising capital and marketing their products during this period.

The Brav and Gompers study also shows that while there is no difference in the performance of small IPO and non-IPO firms, there is a difference between the performance of companies backed by venture capital and those that were not. They found that the firms with venture capital backing significantly outperformed the others. Brav and Gompers conclude that for small companies, IPO and non-IPO companies are relatively similar. What is important is the amount of venture capital an IPO brings to the table when it goes public.

In 1997, Katherine Spiess and Richard Pettway studied the initial discounting of IPO firms, as measured by the mean difference between the initial offer price to the close of first-day trading for each IPO. Their research tested the hypothesis that firms discount the price of the IPO to send a signal that they are a high-quality firm and to get a better response to subsequent equity offerings they have planned.

Spiess and Pettway examined 172 firms that issued IPOs between 1987 and 1991 and then made another equity offering within three years of the IPO. The measurement of initial discounting was the difference between the initial day offering price at opening (not the subscription price) and the initial day's closing price. Firms that had been planning to go public for a long time, that treated the IPO as more than a one time event, did recover the cost of the discounted IPO and often far exceeded the expectations of the company and investors alike. The companies that had not planned carefully and treated the IPO as purely a financing opportunity did not even recover the cost of the discounted IPO.

Raghuram Rajan and Henri Servaes (1997) studied a sample of IPOs issued between 1985 and 1995, looking at the effects of analyst following for IPOs. They found that the longer the company spent readying itself for the IPO, the greater the number of analysts that followed the stock. They also found that these analysts tended to have higher estimates of future earnings of these companies, which caused more investors to purchase the stock. On average, though, these companies did outperform companies that did not go through the same preparation.

Rajan and Servaes hypothesize that the analysts overestimated future earnings of the companies because many of them worked for investment banks with strong relationships with the companies they followed and were therefore biased when asked to project a company's future earnings. Rajan and Servaes believe that long-term preparation for an IPO is a proven way for the company to attract initial capital through the prospects for future growth.

Douglas A. Hensler, Ronald C. Rutherford, and Thomas M. Springer (1997) looked at the survival rates of IPOs in terms of the factors that influence IPO aftermarket performance. Their study showed that because larger IPOs produce greater resources, they are able to withstand a decline better than smaller IPOs. Older company age, initial return, IPO activity, and amount of insider ownership all contributed to the performance of IPOs.

Each of these studies provide insight into why IPOs underperform or overperform expectations, useful information in choosing strategies for approaching investors.

SUMMARY

The research reviewed consistently found that IPO companies initially underprice the value of their shares. However, the findings related to the long-run performance of IPOs are not consistent.

Nothing stays the same. We live in a world of constant and ever-accelerating change. Business conditions are changing so fast that the challenge for a company is to stay ahead of the curve, constantly reevaluating the company's strategy.

The IPO process is cyclical. From time to time, a company will go back and start again. However, each time the company as a whole will approach the process from a more sophisticated perspective. Generally, the first step, the best place to begin, is to define success.

After an IPO, the company is held accountable to many new definitions of success, those of shareholders, the board, customers, the management team, Wall Street analysts, and the press. The ongoing challenge of being a public company is to juggle all these interests, satisfying the needs of all stakeholders while at the same time driving the company ahead. The company's general goal at this point is to keep the momentum up, continuing to build the organization by aggressively managing the following cost drivers:

- Intellectual capital.
- Talent capital.
- Value-chain capital.
- Financial capital.

As with raising a child, managing a public company can be both challenging and deeply rewarding, nurturing the company, watching it grow, financing its needs, not to mention providing discipline when necessary. With the proper balance between caring attention, intelligent thought, informed advice, and good luck, the company will mature into an entity that is healthy, strong, and prosperous.

CHAPTER 5

ALTERNATIVE SOURCES OF FINANCING

As part of the process of deciding whether and when to go public, a company will want to consider not only the costs and consequences of a public offering but also the relative merits of alternative sources of financing. Which route is chosen will depend on the urgency of the company's financial need, corporate and shareholder objectives, the amount of capital needed, the use to which the proceeds will be applied, and the relative size and maturity of the company. Loughran and Ritter (1995) analyzed some alternatives to going public:

PRIVATE PLACEMENTS AND LIMITED OFFERINGS

The SEC has established exemptions from federal registration for sales of securities that meet certain conditions. These conditions relate to the amount of capital raised (up to $1 million, up to $5 million, or unlimited) and the number and financial sophistication of investors who purchase the securities (from an unlimited number to only 35 "non-accredited" investors and unlimited "accredited" investors). Other conditions relate to advertising, disclosure requirements, and resale restrictions. A financial specialist or a securities lawyer can help the company work through whether and how it can meet the conditions for these particular alternatives. In a private placement, no general solicitation is allowed and marketing is limited to qualified investors that have a pre-existing relationship with the company or broker soliciting the sale. The advantages and disadvantages of the applicable rules are:

- **Rule 505**

  Advantages: Up to 35 unsophisticated investors and an unlimited number of accredited investors can be sold securities. No federal review is required and the offering may be exempt from many state reviews.

  Disadvantages: Capital raised is limited to $5 million in 12 months. No general solicitation is permitted and professional investors may request onerous terms due to illiquidity.

- **Rule 506/Section 452**

  Advantages: An unlimited dollar amount can be sold to 35 sophisticated and experienced investors, and an unlimited number of accredited investors. No federal review is required and the offering may be exempt from many state reviews.

  Disadvantages: No general solicitation is permitted and professional investors may extract onerous terms due to illiquidity.

INTRASTATE OFFERINGS

To promote local financing of local business, the SEC exempts from registration offerings made only to the residents of the state in which the issuer resides and carries on its business. The amount raised and the number of investors are not restricted but a number of other conditions are imposed. The company must be incorporated in the state and must carry out a significant portion of its business there. All the purchasers must be residents of the state and their right to sell the shares they buy to out-of-state investors is restricted. Although SEC registration requirements do not apply to an intrastate offering, a company going this route must still meet the requirements of the state securities law.

COMMERCIAL LENDERS AND LESSORS

Loans from banks, insurance companies and other financial institutions and lease financing of equipment are the most common ways to raise capital. The relative ease of obtaining a bank loan or lease financing makes these sources well suited to meeting short-term working capital needs and investing in new equipment. Semipermanent capital to purchase real property or to make acquisitions may also be available from lenders, but lenders and lessors may require collateral or even personal guarantees from the principals of the company. The company also may have to meet certain financial conditions while the debt or lease is outstanding. Debt financing also commits a company to cash outflows that may be hard to meet if interest rates climb or if the business declines.

STRATEGIC PARTNERSHIPS

A company can obtain the resources to meet its economic and strategic goals by forming an alliance with a larger, financially stronger company. A strategic partnership can contribute more than money to a company's success. For example, a partner might provide manufacturing or technological capabilities or give the company access to new or expanded distribution channels.

EMPLOYEE STOCK OWNERSHIP PLANS

Consider an employee stock ownership plan (ESOP) if, in addition to raising capital, the company's goals include increased liquidity, personal tax and estate planning for the principals, and employee motivation. An ESOP is a tax-favored type of employee benefit plan that is a vehicle for employee ownership of a company. The ESOP is allowed to borrow money to buy the company's stock and maintain it for the employees' retirement.

GOVERNMENT LOANS AND GUARANTEES

Although subject to a variety of qualifications, restrictions, and delays, government loans and guarantees are often a very attractive source of financing. Some very reasonable rates and payment schedules can be obtained. These programs sometimes represent the only available source of financing from both start-up small businesses and larger businesses falling on hard times. A variety of programs are available at the federal, state, and local levels.

An example of an agency, which would finance such a program, would include the U.S. Small Business Administration (SBA). The SBA is an independent agency of the Executive Branch of the Federal Government. The SBA sets the guidelines for the loans and guarantees that some of the risk to its lending partners, community development organizations and micro-lending institutions, will be eliminated.

VENTURE CAPITALISTS

Raising capital through venture capitalists or other institutional equity investors can be either the first step in going public or an alternative to going public. Venture capitalists typically will agree to provide a significant portion of a company's capital needs but in return they require a significant, often a controlling, equity interest in the business and direct representation on the board of directors. They typically invest in businesses with relatively high risk in the hope of high returns. Their involvement in management of the company can range from passive monitoring of the results to hands-on involvement in day-to-day operations. Financing from a venture capitalist almost invariably results in ownership dilution and often in eventual if not immediate loss of control.

SALE OR MERGER

If the company's motivation for considering a public offering is to liquidate the business investment, selling or merging the company may be an attractive alternative. Other corporations or the company's current management team may be attracted to the opportunity. The decision to sell depends on the personal goals of the owners, but this option is often an excellent way to maximize returns.

CHAPTER 6

IS THE COMPANY READY?

WHAT INVESTORS WILL LOOK FOR

There is no formula or universal rule to determine whether a company is sufficiently large, mature, or profitable to go public, but a review of recent successful offerings illuminates some useful generalizations about what investors look for in a newly public company.

SIZE

Underwriters have their own rules of thumb, based primarily on revenue and net earnings, for what constitutes adequate company size to support a public offering. Today, however, size is often measured in terms of market capitalization or float.

If a company appears to lack the sales volume or the earnings to support a successful public offering, there are other avenues to explore. Management might look for another company in the same industry that also is too small for an IPO. The result could be an amalgamated company whose combined assets, earnings, and management make a public offering feasible.

GROWTH

Underwriters and investors look for a consistent record of high growth as well as demonstrated potential for continuing that growth in the future. That means growth of 15 to 25 percent per year for the next several years. Unless a company has that kind of momentum going when it goes public, investors will turn to more promising opportunities and the offering may fizzle. An innovative product, significant market share, or proven potential in a new market that is part of an emerging industry all contribute to the company's real and perceived prospects for growth.

PROFITABILITY

Many companies that have successful IPOs have a track record of stable revenue and earnings. In exceptional cases where companies have excellent earnings trend lines, investors may trade off prospects for exceptional growth and price appreciation for lower risk and a reliable dividend stream.

There are no hard-and-fast rules. Each company must evaluate its present circumstances and its prospects, bearing in mind that few elements in the overall picture will impress the investor as much as momentum. Nevertheless, every year, start-up companies in "glamour" or "hot" industries go public. Many of these companies have never posted a profit. Some have never even reported revenues.

Although a positive trend line is optimal, it certainly is not always necessary. Even mature companies with aberrations in their earnings trends have successfully executed their IPO strategies, particularly if the aberration was caused by some unusual, one-time, or nonrecurring change that is unlikely to affect future operating results. In the final analysis, the critical success factor is not short-term earnings but the ability to sustain financial performance over the long term.

MANAGEMENT CAPABILITIES

Underwriters and investors carefully consider size, growth, and profitability in evaluating a company but weaknesses in any of these areas will not necessarily preclude a public offering. The issue on which underwriters and investors are most reluctant to compromise is management strength. Strong management thus translates into the most important intangible element in any IPO investor confidence.

Senior executives must be painfully honest in analyzing whether they can comfortably adjust to public scrutiny of their actions on behalf of the company. Are they ready to cope with the inevitable loss of freedom and privacy? Are they ready to admit outsiders to the decision-making process? Do they have the leadership capability to grow as the company grows?

THE PLAN FOR USING THE IPO PROCEEDS

Part of being prepared for an IPO is for the company to have a clear strategy for communicating with underwriters, investors, and employees its reasons for undertaking the IPO. The success of the process will depend on the coherence and the credibility of the story the company tells. Investors are looking for a compelling reason why the company is raising funds in the public market. Generating more working capital is not a compelling reason. Highly successful companies have a clearly articulated and persuasive plan for what they will do with the proceeds of the IPO.

If a plan for using the proceeds is not self-evident, the first step is to review the initiatives in the business plan. Can the company use the proceeds to reposition the company strategy? to reengineer processes? to reconfigure the infrastructure? to revitalize the culture? One strategy the market looks favorably is a plan to use recapitalization to pay off debt.

The company needs to evaluate its projected use of the proceeds from the perspective of whether the proposed initiative creates high or low shareholder value, as well as whether the value created will be long or short-term.

CORPORATE HOUSEKEEPING

Before the company proceeds into an IPO, some corporate housekeeping may be necessary. This begins with an analysis of whether the current corporate, capital, and management structures are appropriate for a public company and whether the company's transactions with its owners and managers have been properly documented.

Corporate housekeeping begins early in the planning stage and may not be completed until the registration statement is filed with the SEC. The following are typical questions to be considered:

- *Should additional shares be authorized?* More shares might be needed not only for the public offering but also for future acquisitions.

- *Should the capital structure be changed?* Restructuring may have tax implications. Any tax disadvantages can be mitigated with appropriate planning. A company may want to simplify restructuring by issuing common shares in exchange for preferred stock or special classes of common stock.

- *Should the stock be split before the company goes public?* To improve marketability of their common stock, companies frequently split their stock, after consulting with underwriters so that the offering price of the stock will fall between $10 and $20 per share.

- *Should affiliated companies be combined?* A public company generally is organized as a single corporation, though perhaps with subsidiaries. Affiliated companies might provide services to each other, might compete with each other, or might sell related products and services. The combined entity may well be more attractive to investors and thus command a higher price.

- *Should the article of incorporation or bylaws be amended?* A private company may have special voting provisions that are inappropriate for a public company, or the board of directors may need to set up certain committees, such as audit and compensation committees.

- *Are the company's stock records accurate and current?* Accurate shareholder information is a must for a public company.

- *Are the company's transactions or arrangements with owners and managers appropriate for a public company, and are they adequately documented?* The SEC requires public companies to fully disclose all significant related-party transactions. Such transactions should be identified and discussed with legal counsel early in the process.

•*Are the company's contractual obligations appropriate for a public company?* Legal counsel can assist in answering this question by performing a legal audit of significant contracts, among them employment contracts, stock option or purchase plans, debt and lease agreements, shareholder or management loans, rights of first refusal, corporate charter and bylaws, and major supply contracts.

• *Should a stock option' plan be implemented?* An ancillary question is whether additional options should be granted under existing plans.

• *Are important contracts arid employment agreements in writ - ing?* Do they need to be amended?

WERE OTHER COMPANIES READY?

In Appendix A, I discuss both the first-day and long-term performance of IPO companies. First-day underpricing and subsequent long term performance have been well documented by a variety of researchers. Surprisingly, though, I did not find the significant first day underpricing that has been found by researchers like as Garfinkel (1993), Barry and Jennings (1993), and Buser and Chan (1992). In fact, I found the opposite. First-day return for IPOs on average was lower than that of similar non-IPO companies, though not significantly. I believe there are two possible reasons for these apparently contradictory findings:

1. Past research examined IPOs issued during the 1980s but not those issued more recently.

2. My study only covered IPOs issued during a three-year period. Other study periods may reflect IPO performance during different economic cycles.

The results of the t-test indicate that the difference between the initial performance of the IPO companies studied versus the similar non-

IPOs studied was not significant, so no market anomaly was detected.

As with other IPO performance studies, this study found that the long-term results of the IPOs analyzed underperformed the similar non-IPO group, which suggests that companies are not currently implementing the balanced scorecard approach to making an IPO. This does not paint an attractive picture for those thinking of investing in IPO stocks for the long term.

Still, the t-test performed on the mean long-term returns shows that the difference between the two types of companies studied was not significant. The efficient market hypothesis being tested once again held true. The performance of the two groups was not different enough to produce any abnormal gains to investors.

Other studies, such as Buser and Chan (1992), compared IPO performance to benchmarks like the S&P 500 or the Nasdaq. In their study, the Nasdaq Composite Index was used as the benchmark. In my study of all IPOs issued during a given time period, not all IPOs analyzed cleanly matched up with the Nasdaq Composite Index. Doing matchups would be far less time consuming, but I believe less accurate. That is why firm-by-firm matching was used. Only by matching each IPO to its closest non-IPO peer can a reasonable conclusion be drawn with regard to differences in performance.

The siren song of the public market can be strong indeed. Every year, hundreds of companies are drawn to the market by its many significant benefits. Guided by experienced, aggressive management teams and supported by a strong cast of professional advisors, many of these companies parlay their new capital into unprecedented growth.

But going public is not a panacea. Many tales of plunging share prices accompanied by litigation conflicts, management shakeouts, and loss of control counterbalance the fairy-tale success stories. Some companies would have failed anyway but others could have avoided disaster. Executives may find the dimensions and rigors of managing a public company daunting. Poor market timing and lack of adequate planning and preparation also can jeopardize an IPO.

In short, going public can provide many benefits and opportunities but the cost can be substantial, which is why managers and owners must think carefully about whether the company is really ready for an IPO.

CHAPTER 7

TAX PLANNING FOR THE MANAGER

THE PERSONAL CONTEXT

The company is on a success track to an IPO, and the management and founders are the catalysts. But amid the enthusiasm to take the company public, each manager needs to set aside time to focus on how the IPO will affect his or her own personal financial situation. The IPO presents the manager with a unique opportunity to preserve and to create wealth because the company's value will increase dramatically. This is the time to minimize income tax liability and to protect the assets with careful planning. Yet a recent survey (Tech, 1998) found that an astonishing 75 percent of senior executives surveyed did not have a personal wealth management strategy.

Planning early for the personal effects of the potential IPO should be at the heart of the manager's strategy. The manager might consider, for instance, gifting company stock to heirs and setting up certain types of trusts well in advance of the company going public. This can save considerably on estate and gift taxes. It's estimated that every dollar of appreciation that can be removed from a taxable estate could save $0.55 cents in estate taxes.

EFFECTIVE ESTATE TAX PLANNING

The key to successful estate planning is to transfer assets to beneficiaries so that estate or gift tax (often called "transfer tax liability") is minimized. One of the most effective ways to accomplish this is to give away assets that have a low current value but that the manager expects will increase dramatically in value in the future. Stock in a closely held company that may be the subject of a public offering is just that sort of asset.

A federal estate tax is imposed on an estate upon the death of the holder. A gift tax is also imposed on the transfer of assets of more than $11,000 per person annually while an individual is alive. Both of these taxes are imposed at the same rate and are cumulative. This means that when one dies, all previous taxable gifts are added to the estate and the tax is calculated on that amount. The unified transfer tax rate range from 18 percent up to 55 percent.

To limit or completely avoid the amount of tax that must be paid, whether by a manager and by heirs, the estate owner will generally want to depress the value of the assets transferred. The idea is to freeze the value when calculating taxes while retaining the true economic value.

Because assets transferred to beneficiaries or to a favorite charity may be difficult to value, an expert appraisal is a critical element of a successful valuation freeze for transfer tax purposes. An effective appraisal is one that takes advantage of all available discounts yet will be likely to withstand a challenge by the Internal Revenue Service.

Property that trades on an established market can be easily valued. For example, publicly traded stocks and bonds are valued based on the average of the high and low selling prices on the date of a gift or at time of death (or, if the executor chooses, six months after death). However, interests in partnerships and closely held businesses, such as a company before it goes public, must generally be appraised by taking into account the business's assets, earning capacity, and other factors.

ESTATE AND GIFT TAXES

Giving gifts keeps the value of an estate down. The goal from a tax point of view is to keep the valuation of the estate as low as possible, particularly if the estate is larger than $3 million and thus subject to a

55 percent tax rate. (There is an additional 5 percent tax on taxable estates larger than $10 million.)

ANNUAL GIFT TAX EXCLUSION

The law allows an annual gift tax exclusion of $11,000 per donee. A married couple together can thus give up to a $22,000 exclusion per donee. You can thus give $11,000 worth of stock to as many separate people as you want every year without incurring any gift tax consequences.

The annual exclusion can be especially useful if the value of the property gifted can be reduced for gift tax purposes. If shares are worth $110 each, you could give, say, each grandchild 100 shares, but you could give 200 shares if the value were reduced to $55. If you plan to give gifts of stock in your company in the same year as the company is planning an IPO, then, it is wisest to make the gift well in advance of the IPO, on the assumption that the value will rise after the IPO and you would then be able to give fewer shares.

MEDICAL AND EDUCATIONAL EXPENSE EXCLUSIONS

An unlimited gift tax exclusion applies to the payment of medical and educational expenses for any recipient, so long as the payments are made directly to the medical care provider or to the educational institution. The exclusion is especially helpful for someone who wants to help grandchildren or other relatives with their private school or college tuition payments. (Parental support would not be considered a "gift.") Although gifts of stock cannot be used for these purposes, using stock for gifts to other people would free up funds for medical and tuition expenses.

THE MARITAL DEDUCTION

The marital deduction is a feature of both the estate tax and the gift tax. A taxpayer who is married is allowed an unlimited deduction for the value of property transferred to the spouse and neither the spouse nor the estate will be subject to gift or estate tax. The estate tax marital deduction essentially permits paying the estate tax to be postponed until the second spouse dies.

Because of the unlimited marital deduction, many taxpayers commit the common error of leaving everything to their spouses when they die and leaving the spouse to work out who gets what. The problem is that this results in a higher tax when the second spouse dies. It is important, therefore, that each spouse have individually owned assets at least equal to the unified credit equivalent that can be left to other desired beneficiaries, either directly or through a trust.

CREDITS

When calculating the net federal estate tax due, the estate personal representative can claim certain credits against the tax. The best known credit is the unified estate and gift tax credit. It is called a "unified" credit because it applies against both gift and estate taxes, the amount of tax generated by a transfer of $675,000. The amount of the unified credit equivalent is scheduled to rise in the future as follows:

Year(s)	Unified Credit Equivalent
2004	$850,000
2005	$950,000
2006 or thereafter	$1,000,000

Other credits include state and foreign death tax credits and a credit for tax paid on prior transfers. The latter to part or all of the tax paid on property transferred as a gift before a person died or through that person's estate afterward.

INCOME TAX STRATEGIES AND IPOS

Income taxes will play a major role in the decisions made by controlling stockholders when a company goes public. It is possible to minimize those taxes by using legal techniques that allow the stockholders to avoid or to defer them. There are a number of ways to avoid capital gains tax when stock is sold to the public.

CHARITABLE REMAINDER TRUSTS

Managers who sell their interest in a company to the public may be subject to a 20 percent federal capital gains tax on any profit from the sale, in addition to state and local income taxes. One of the most useful vehicles for avoiding at least part of these capital gains taxes is a charitable remainder trust (CRT).

CRTs allow you to maximize tax savings after you sell stock by contributing a portion of the value of the appreciated stock to a favorite charity and a portion (in the form of an annuity) to noncharitable beneficiaries, such as children and grandchildren. Instead of selling the stock directly, the individual transfers the stock into a CRT. The trustee then sells the stock, but because the trust is tax-exempt, no tax is due. The trustee can thus reinvest the pretax proceeds. The trust provides that at least annual payments be made to the individual or any other designated beneficiaries. When the term or lifetime interest ends, the charity will have full use of the entire property. A donor can name a specific charity as the remainder beneficiary when setting up the CRT or decide later on. Some people name their own private foundations as the beneficiary.

Although actual receipt of the funds by the charity is deferred, the donor gets an immediate income tax deduction for the present value of the interest that passes to charity. Later the trust assets will be included in the donor's taxable estate, but there will be an estate tax charitable deduction for the value of what goes to charity.

POOLED INCOME FUNDS

Another form of charitable giving that shares many of the tax effects of a CRT is a pooled income fund in which donors place their gifts to a fund with gifts from others that is managed by a charity. Each donor receives a pro rata share of the pooled income fund's earnings for life. After the donor dies, the principle contributed goes to the charity.

Pooling of funds makes it easier to diversify investments, making it possible to afford more expert management than a trust can afford. As with a CRT, when the fund sells the stock, there is no tax liability. The distinction is that the managers of the fund, rather than the trustee of a trust, retain investment discretion.

MINIMIZING INCOME TAXES IN THE IPO YEAR

Income taxes in the IPO year can be minimized through a Charitable Lead Trust (CLT), and additional tax deductions and tax saving strategies.

THE CHARITABLE LEAD TRUST

A charitable lead trust (CLT) is the mirror image of a CRT. In this case, the charity gets the interest, and the noncharitable beneficiary gets the principal at a certain point. CLTs can be used for either estate or income tax planning purposes. They may generate a large up-front income tax deduction for the donor or a low-taxed transfer to beneficiaries. If a CLT is set up properly, the charity gets the income or lead interest and the remainder interest (whatever is left in the trust when it terminates) returns to the donor or passes to chosen beneficiaries.

If the remainder interest reverts to the donor, he or she may claim a current charitable income tax deduction equal to the present value of the income stream, but the trust income will be included in the donor's income as the charity receives it and the remainder will be part of the estate. This can result in a large income tax deduction in the year the CLT is set up. If the remainder interest passes to beneficiaries other than a charity, there may be no up-front charitable deduction, but usually the income will not be taxable and the value of the beneficiary's remainder interest will be low.

OTHER TAX DEDUCTIONS

In the company's IPO year, members of the management team will probably be in the highest tax bracket they have yet achieved. Clearly, this is the time to take advantage of as many tax deductions as possible. A manager may want to accelerate deductions into that year because the value of a deduction is more when the tax bracket is higher. Consider making outright charitable gifts of company stock after the IPO, you can get a full-market-value deduction without having to recognize any gain.

Many entrepreneurs establish a private family foundation or directed gift fund with a company stock contribution. This allows the benefits of charitable giving to extend to the future generations. Another option is to accelerate the payment of other deductible expenses such as investment interest, mortgage interest, real estate and state and local income taxes, and investment expenses.

OTHER TAX SAVING STRATEGIES

A number of other tax saving strategies are worth looking into:

- Investing in tax-exempt securities.
- Realizing capital losses to offset the gain realized on the IPO.

- Maximizing the use of tax-deferral vehicles, such as qualified retirement plans, nonqualified deferred compensation, life insurance, and annuities.
- Taking advantage of the lower tax brackets of children to make gifts.

As with estate planning, the critical consideration is that the taxpayer begin planning well in advance of the actual IPO so that tax affairs can be structured in a rational and unhurried manner and that potential IRS challenges to the substance of any transactions are avoided or mitigated.

OPTIMIZING INVESTMENTS

Once a manager has converted what was an illiquid asset into cash by selling stock in the public market, a major concern is what to do with that cash. Because all investments are subject to some risk and many returns vary widely from year to year, what is the best way to get the return needed with an affordable amount of risk? The answer is to diversify investments so that you're not putting all your eggs in one basket. Someone who has gone through an IPO probably still has a large position in the company stock. The cash received from selling the other shares should thus be diversified out of the company and probably out of that industry or market segment.

The shareholder is well advised to consult a financial advisor to help make sure his or her investments achieve the level of diversity desired to minimize risk. Choosing a money manager is clearly something that must be done carefully. Investigate several people. Find out what their investment track record is. What type of return does this person typically achieve on investments for other clients? Ask for references, to check them. A money manager for personal assets has to be just as qualified as the underwriter for the company's IPO.

CONCLUSION

Perhaps the most important bit of advice here is that the pre-IPO tax and personal financial planning process should begin well before the manager starts the company's IPO planning. Those who wait until shortly before going public to set up a trust (and there are many kinds other than the ones mentioned here that might be useful) or even just to make outright gifts to beneficiaries are risking higher valuations than they would have had just a year earlier. Valuation of a private company works its way up the closer the date of the IPO. Higher valuations result in higher gift and transfer taxes.

It is critical that controlling stockholders and executives in a private company considering an IPO place as much importance on their personal financial situations as on the company's financial situation. The decision they make should reflect their own personal values, not someone else's idea of what is appropriate. An executive dedicated to helping the homeless may make a homeless shelter the remainder beneficiary of a charitable trust. One who strongly believes that the children need the advice of a money manager can place a gift to them in a trust so that a trustee will oversee its management. In all cases, seek sound, objective advice of investment and tax consultants.

CHAPTER 8

ARE WE THERE YET?

The market for IPOs has varied dramatically, from the depressed levels of the mid-1970, when fewer than 50 companies a year went public, to the record highs of over 500 companies a year in the early 1990s. In deciding whether this is the right time to go public, one of the critical questions to ask is about the mood of the market is right (Jan, 1997). Is it market slumping or strong? Are prices falling or rising? Is trading volume down or up?

Market conditions can change rapidly. Many factors influence the market, political developments, interest rates, inflation, economic forecasts, and sundry other matters that seem (and often are) unrelated to the quality of a company's stock. The market is admittedly emotional. Investors' moods change from bullish to bearish and back again to the consternation of everyone, even the experts.

Investor acceptance of new issues is cyclical but is nevertheless often not predictable. Investor infatuation with a certain industry can significantly increase the share price a company may obtain. However, as we have said, the window for new issues, and for a specific industry in particular, can close just as quickly as it opened.

ADVANCE PLANNING

Planning for a public offering of securities should start as quickly as possible (in case I haven't got that message over yet). Whether the company is considering going public within the next six months or in three years, it will have to consider a variety of factors. Early attention to these considerations can help reduce many of the costs and burdens of an IPO. Starting very early to lay the groundwork on which to build a strong corporate image and long-term investor interest will pay huge dividends in the form of a stronger and more stable aftermarket for the company's shares.

THINGS TO THINK ABOUT

Once a company has decided to go public, it must consider the steps needed to ensure a smooth transition from private to public. It may need to do some corporate house-keeping, even house-cleaning. It will have to determine whether it has the information it needs for the registration statement, and if not, how to assemble it.

Though corporate housekeeping generally begins during the planning stage, it may not be completed until the registration statement is filed with the SEC. It reaches down to very basic levels: Are the current corporate, capital, and management structures appropriate for a public company? Are transactions between owners and management properly documented? The typical questions that need to be answered during this phase are:

- *Should the company's capital structure be charged?*
  Restructuring may have tax implications but any tax disadvantages can be mitigated with careful planning. The company may want to simplify the capital structure, perhaps by issuing common shares in exchange for preferred stock or special classes of common stock.

- *Should additional shares of stock be authorized?* Additional shares might be needed not just for the public offering but also for future acquisitions or similar transactions.

- *Should the stock be split before going public?* To improve marketability of common stock, on the advice of underwriters, companies often split their stock so that the offering price of the stock will be between $10 to $20 per share.

• *Should affiliated companies be combined?* A public company generally is organized as a single corporation, perhaps with subsidiaries. Affiliated companies might provide services to each other, compete with each other, or sell related products and services. The combined entity may well be more attractive to investors and thus command a higher price in the market.

• *Should the articles of incorporation or bylaws be amended?* A private company may have special voting provisions that are inappropriate for a public company, or it might seem desirable to establish certain committees of the board of directors, such as audit and compensation committees.

• *Are the company's stock records accurate and current?* This is a must for a public company.

• *Are transactions or arrangements with owners and members of management appropriate for a public company?* Are they adequately documented? The SEC requires public companies to fully disclose all significant related-party transactions. These should be identified and discussed with legal counsel early in the process. Arrangements with shareholders and officers that may serve a private company well could be considered inappropriate for a public company. Legal counsel can help ensure the appropriateness of any contractual obligations by performing a legal audit of significant contracts, including:
  – Employment contracts. –
  – Stock option or purchase plans.
  – Debt and lease agreements.
  – Shareholder or management loans.
  – Rights of first refusal.
  – Corporate charter and bylaws.
  – Major supply contracts.

Questions a legal audit will ask are:

• Have important contracts and employment agreements been put in writing? Do they need to be amended? Should a stock-option plan be implemented? Should additional options be granted under existing plans?

- Does management have sufficient and experience for a public company? The company may need to supplement or upgrade its financial or operating management before it goes public. Changes in the board of directors are often appropriate (for example, adding outside directors).

EXTERNAL RELATIONSHIPS

Strong relationships with professional advisors can be a significant asset for a private company, but for a public company, they are crucial. It is never too soon to start building those relationships.

At this point, the company should already have an investment banker. If not, now is the time to get one. Some are large, full-service investment banking firms. Others are individuals who specialize in specific industries. Investment bankers can advise on available sources of capital and on the desirability of offering securities at a given time, both with respect to initial offerings in general and in the company's industry in particular. Through them the company can keep its finger on the pulse of the capital markets. Often the same firm that serves as the investment banker can also act as underwriter when the company decides to go public. Therefore, the company should select an investment banker using the same criteria it would use to select underwriters.

COMPANY MANAGEMENT

Preparing to be a public company also may necessitate changes in internal reporting and in how the company is managed. In many private companies, the officers report informally to the president, who makes the final decisions on significant matters. A public company must be managed more formally. The transition to a public company will be more orderly the earlier the company starts to manage its business as if it were a public company.

Selecting the best people to serve on the board of directors can be one of the most important tasks of a company that has decided to go public. This decision can affect both the short and long-term direction of a company, as well as the success of the IPO. Board members will play a key role in assuring the effectiveness of a strategic plan, bringing their experience and new ideas into the company, monitoring the chief executive officer's performance, assuring the integrity of company operations, and counseling top management. In addition, they will directly impact future mergers and acquisitions, tender offers, compensation of top management, selection of senior executives, and many of the company's capital expenditures.

Ideally, the board of directors should begin to play a larger role in policy decisions at least two to three years before the company goes public. This often represents a major change for a company that traditionally has been run by one or a small group of entrepreneurs. However, the change is necessary. It demonstrates to underwriters and investors that the company is stable and mature, and is one indication that a company is less likely to struggle in the new public environment.

As we have already discussed in chapter 3, the board of directors should be structured so as to promote the board's role as an independent and knowledgeable overseer of the company's affairs and performance. There is no single board structure that can be prescribed for all companies that have decided to go public. We have already discussed the many factors that should be considered when assembling a board for a company that is contemplating going public, including the time commitment and legal responsibilities board members must accept and the importance having a balance of specialties represented.

FINANCIAL REPORTING

The prospectus for the company's IPO generally must include audited financial statements for the previous three years, although that requirement is reduced in certain circumstances, such as for small business issuers under Regulation S-B. It also may require selected financial information for the previous five years. These disclosure requirements apply only for years the company has been in existence.

A company usually will not be allowed to go public if its financial statements have not been audited. Sometimes, two- or three-year audits can be performed in anticipation of a public offering but these may cause unforeseen delays and turn up unexpected adjustments to earnings.

Public companies are subject to certain SEC disclosure requirements, such as specified data by industry segment. To prepare for these disclosures, the company should fine-tune its financial reporting system to provide the necessary data, which should in any case be reviewed by the auditors. Many internal reporting systems already provide industry segment data in some form, but the method they use may not correspond to the one prescribed by the SEC or by Statement No. 14, "Segment Reporting" issued by the Financial Accounting Standards Board (FASB). By making the necessary changes in accounting practices early, the company can avoid the inconvenience of having to implement them when they will distract from the IPO, or, worse, having to delay the offering.

A company also can run into problems if, in the two or three years preceding a public offering, it acquires a significant business that was not previously audited. Because the financial statements of unaudited subsidiaries affect the consolidated financial statements, and also because of the SEC requirement of separate audited financial statements for significant acquired companies, a company that makes such an acquisition may not be able to go public until the needed audits are done. Any company that is planning a public offering of securities in the next two or three years will want to keep SEC audit requirements in mind when considering any acquisitions.

Many private companies have annual audits even if they are not otherwise required. This puts them in a position to go public on short notice. An audit improves the credibility and reliability of the company's financial statements and will help in dealings with external lenders and suppliers and improve internal management.

Another benefit is that an independent auditor who is knowledgeable about the business may come up with creative solutions to the business needs of the company. These ideas, whether communicated in personal meeting or in management letters, can lead to cost-effective ways to improve internal controls. Effective and timely internal financial reporting and a good system of internal controls may be crucial for public companies but they are also highly important for a private company.

In addition to their professional and advisory services, the auditors will help determine whether the accounting practices used are appropriate for a public company. Sometimes, SEC interpretations of GAAP may necessitate a change in accounting practices and disclosures by a company about to go public. Alternatively, companies may desire to conform their accounting policies to those more commonly used by other public companies in their industry and thereby to enhance the value of the IPO. By making the necessary changes early, a company can avoid the distractions of having to do so as it goes public. Such changes may also have tax implications that need to be taken into account.

Once the company is publicly held, the SEC sets limits on the sale of "restricted" stock, generally shares issued in private placements and shares held by controlling shareholders. Existing shareholders may sell any portion of their holdings without technical restriction as part of the IPO, the only "restriction" then is a practical concern that the offering not be perceived as a bailout of existing shareholders. However, if one of the goals of the public offering is to make the shares of controlling shareholders salable in the aftermarket, advance planning can reduce the impact of these SEC restrictions (Hensler, Rutherford, and Springer, 1997).

A YEAR BEFORE THE OFFERING

Selling the company's shares and maintaining investor interest in the aftermarket is much like selling a product or services to customers. Both are enhanced by name recognition, advertising and publicity, a product support system, and good distribution channels. The company's underwriter and the underwriting syndicate constitute the distribution channel, but the company itself will need to create a recognizable corporate image and build the foundation for a strong investor relations program.

Creating the right corporate image takes time. It should be begun well in advance of the public offering. Bear in mind, too, the SEC restrictions on advertising or publicity once the registration process has been started.

The first step in creating public image is to perform a thorough self-evaluation that takes into account the geography of the market (regional or national), the industry in which the company will be categorized (if there's a choice, pick the one with most appeal to investors), and the products that will lead the charge. What this all boils down to is a single question: What corporate image does the company want to project?

The next question is: To whom? Think about whether the company will mainly be appealing to retail or institutional investors, and which large segments of these should be targeted by an image-building program.

Once the target market of investors has been determined and the corporate image the company wishes to project, the company must find ways to reach that market. Unless the company has substantial in-house public relations resources, it might be wise to hire a financial public relations firm and consult its own advertising agencies about what media will work best, given the image-building goals.

It will be necessary to make a special effort to reach the securities analysts and members of the business media who speak to the customer segments the company wants to reach. It never hurts to have a good relationship with the press, both trade publications and the national or local business and financial press.

COMPENSATION STRATEGIES

Even if the company considers its compensation plan to be highly effective, the plan should be reexamined in preparation for its IPO. Although a company can, and in many cases should, preserve elements of the plan, it will need to adapt them to suit its new status as a public company.

Going public gives companies a powerful new element for their compensation plans, publicly traded equity that can be used to enhance compensation in the form of both outright stock grants and stock options. On the other hand, a company will be making compensation decisions in a much more public arena. In this new environment, the company will need to communicate its pay policies not only to employees, but also to regulators, investors, stock exchange officials, and the public at large.

INTERNAL CONTROLS

Most companies, public and private, have long recognized the importance of strong internal controls. An effective internal control structure is essential if companies are to achieve their financial goals, prevent loss of resources, and prepare reliable financial statements.

Companies considering an IPO need to take a close look at their systems of internal control to evaluate how effectively they can deliver the information regulators will require. As we explained in Chapter 3, legislation like the Foreign Corrupt Practices Act of 1977 makes it imperative that a public company have systems in place to document all transactions accurately and limit access to assets.

PREPARING A BUSINESS PLAN

Whether the company decides to go public or to pursue alternative financing, it cannot succeed without a sound business plan (Leedy, 1997). A business plan is a valuable management tool that can be used in any case in a wide variety of situations beyond simply financing. In most companies, business plans are used at minimum to:

- Set the goals and objectives for company performance.

- Provide a basis for evaluating and controlling company perform-ance.

- Communicate company goals and message to middle managers and other employees, outside directors, suppliers, lenders, and potential investors.

SETTING GOALS AND OBJECTIVES

The business plan for an early-stage company is in many ways a first attempt at strategic planning. An entrepreneur should use a business plan to help set the direction of a company over the next several years. The plan should define the action steps that will be taken and the processes that will be used to guide the company through this period.

Many entrepreneurs say that the pressures of the day-to-day management of a company leave them little time for planning. This is not only short-sighted, it is unfortunate. Without planning, an owner runs the risk of proceeding blindly while the business environment changes rapidly around him. Writing a business plan does not guarantee a particular business environment, nor is it a guarantee that problems will not arise, but, with a thoroughly thought-out plan, the business owner is in a better position to anticipate a crisis and deal with it before it destroys the business. Further, a well-constructed plan may help avoid certain problems altogether. In fact, business planning is probably more important to the survival of a small and growing company than a larger, more mature one.

A business plan can also be used to identify and document achievement of milestones along a company's business path to success. In the heat of daily operations, a company will find it difficult to take an objective look at how the business is doing, the trees encountered daily obscure the view of the forest in which the company operates. A business plan is a map through the forest. It gives the management team an objective basis for determining whether the business is on track to reach the goals and objectives it has set.

Financial statements and projections for the next three to five years generally are part of the business plan. Financial modeling can be used to present alternative "what-if" scenarios. This is the point of the business plan, to specify on sound reasoning how much money a company needs, how it will be used, how much the company needs when, whether the company might need more, and when and how the company will repay the money. Some parts of the plan are reasonably easy to prepare. Others require more time and effort, and often some research. The company will want to retain auditors and lawyers to either help prepare or to review the document.

TOPICS TO BE COVERED

Certain fundamental topics addressed in most successful business plans are incorporated into the following outline for a high-tech operation whose sample business plan is given later in the chapter:

I. Executive summary.
    a. Introduction.

    b. Mission.
    c. Keys to success.
II. Company summary.
    a. The management team.
    b. Business services.
    c. User services.
    d. Strategic partners.
    e. Company locations.
III. Services and products.
    a. Services description.
    b. Corporate alliance/strategic partnerships.
    c. Revenue sources.
IV. Background and industry analysis.
V. Market analysis.
    a. Market overview.
    b. Main competitors.
    c. Competitor analysis.
VI. Strategy summary.
    a. Opportunities and benchmarks.
    b. Sales and marketing strategy.
    c. Operating techniques.
VII. Financial history and projections.
    a. Financing requirements.
    b. Financial information.

SAMPLE FIVE-YEAR BUSINESS PLAN

Following is the sample business plan of a fictitious company, including the steps outlined above.

EXECUTIVE SUMMARY

R-Data (RD) plans to sell real time market research data that profiles Internet users and the Web sites they browse. This highly desirable marketing data will be accumulated from a large base of RD users by enhancing the proven user-incentive program of free Internet access. Users will not only be given free dial-up access to the Internet but will also have the opportunity to earn additional incentives if they further interact with RD software. Using an innovative software application that interacts with the user's Web browser, RD will capture site and user statistics in real-time. RD will accumulate statistics such as the total number of visitors to a Web site at any time ("Web audience"), their demographic data, individual Web surfing habits and preferences, and much more.

Given that 80 percent of Internet users are willing to provide personal information in return for a customized surfing experience, we are confident that we will be able to create an environment that will persuade our users to be forthcoming with useful, pertinent, cutting-edge marketing data. Our RD software package will accomplish this in part by allowing users to personalize their Web surfing experience, which will give RD even greater insight into users' Web browsing habits. RD business clients will be able to purchase this highly valued information and will have the option of interacting in real-time with the users browsing any Web site.

COMPANY OVERVIEW

R-Data (RD) is in the business of gathering valuable personal information about Web browsers using the latest in technology. Clients will be able to conduct on-line surveys and direct their advertising to a targeted Web audience. Thus, by collecting background information about Web users, RD will in essence provide a market for the seller to court the buyer. We believe that our business philosophy is best explained in our mission statement and keys to success.

MISSION

RD offers highly desirable marketing data to businesses for market research and business analysis. RD's business clients will be able to purchase highly valued information and have the option of interacting with Internet-browsing users in real-time. RD will maintain financial balance, placing a high value for its services and delivering an even higher value to its clients.

KEYS TO SUCCESS

RD's strategy for success includes:

- A commitment to excellence in fulfilling its promises. RD will offer completely confidential, reliable, trustworthy expertise and Internet marketing data information to business clients and users.

- A highly focused marketing team to generate new business leads.

- A single pool of expertise into multiple revenue-generation opportunities—access real-time marketing data, communicate real-time with Web audiences, generate market research reports, and consult on marketing projects.

- Web site and Web user statistics captured in real-time.

BUSINESS ENVIRONMENT

Both on-line advertisements and e-commerce sales are growing at a staggering rate. One indicator, Business Week's "Info Tech 100," recognizes companies that have proved their ability to translate premium digital-business-building expertise and high consumer satisfaction into solid business performance. Being named to such lists, and topping them, is an RD goal. Business Week uses financial data from Standard & Poor's Compustat, which has on 100,000 publicly traded companies, ranking the top 200 information companies based upon revenues, revenue growth in percentage, return on equity, total return, and profits. Companies that did not increase revenues at a pace concurrent with their industry's average were eliminated from the rankings. Among the industry leaders listed in 2002 "Info Tech 100" were:

AOL
Apple Computer
Microsoft
Nokia
Nvidia
Oracle

BACKGROUND AND INDUSTRY ANALYSIS

The phenomenon known as the Internet has established itself within our society and has extensively broadened its niche within a relatively short time. Over the span of just about 20 years, the Internet has come to completely dominate the attention of entrepreneurs as well as common citizens. This technological powerhouse known as the Net was actually born from an attempt by the U.S. Defense Department to connect its own network, called the ARPAnet, with other radio and satellite networks. ARPAnet was an experimental network designed to support strategic military research—in particular, research on how to build additional networks that could still function despite attack from, for instance, bombs.

The concept that revolutionized our models of communication, as well as affecting nearly every realm within any modernized society, was that every computer within the respective network could "talk" with any other. From this quite simple idea, the Internet was born.

How could the Internet grow so quickly to have the influential impact it now boasts? One theory analogizes the Internet to a cloud that seems small from our limited point of reference but actually extends for miles. Every time a connection to the Internet is made, whether it is in the privacy of home or at the workplace, the Internet is extended. The investment and activity by small, medium, and large organizations to extend the Internet just a few miles each to office location dwarfs all that was ever done with ARPAnet by a ratio of millions to one.

In more recent years, there has been a growing impetus for internet service providers to build their own infrastructure. For instance, IBM created GlobalNet, which links about 20,000 businesses currently, and Netcom has a network linking about 68 cities.

As will be seen below, R-Data will have major competitors on both aspects of its work, acquiring users with a reward-based program and selling Internet marketing intelligence to businesses. However, no competitor to date can provide the services RD will offer to its users. Though these two industries may seem to have existed for some time, both are actually relatively young, only about two years old. However, extremely large growth in both is predicted for the next few years and data from 1999–2002 support the notion that the high growth trend will continue for years to come. These industries are directly related to online ad spending and e-commerce growth, which bodes well up for rising companies with innovative ideas, like R-Data. The World Wide online advertisement market is a $6.5 billion industry. E-commerce, according to International Data Corp., already has reached $200 billion in volume.

Currently, many companies are offering Internet users rewards to entice them to use their services. Some companies offer free Internet access, monthly checks based on usage, or credit at a partner's e-tailer shop in exchange for varying degrees of interaction. Unfortunately, some Internet business models, such as the free Internet access model that relies solely on ad banner revenue, have failed. Although some corporations have stood the test of time, the experience of others illustrates that success requires more than simply creating a company that parallels or utilizes the Internet.

Several companies dominate the free Internet access industry (Table 9-1):

TABLE 9-1
TOP INDUSTRY LEADERS—2002

COMPANY	NUMBER OF USERS (IN MILLIONS)
AllAdvantage	5
NetZero	3
1stUp	1

All three are still relatively young and waiting to mature, expand, to grow.

The Internet marketing intelligence industry also has many segments. The segment that most closely competes with R-Data's revenue sources is Web traffic measuring, where there are four major competitors (1) Media Metrix, (2) NetRatings, (3) PC Data Inc., and (4) Web Side Story. The first three companies have proprietary software that measures Web traffic through a select control group. Web Side Story, on the other hand, provides businesses with detailed information on visitors to the businesses' own Web sites. R-Data will differ from other companies within the Web traffic measuring market because it will not have the limitations its competitors have placed on themselves.

MARKET TRENDS

Forrester Research predicts that on-line ad revenue alone will rise from $3.3 billion in 2002 to $33 billion in 2005. Revenues for R-Data are expected to double from $111 billion in 2002 to $217 billion in the year

2003. With such rapid growth in spending, businesses will surely demand better use of their advertising dollar. Competition within the on-line advertisement industry will also intensify as competitors try to outdo each other in reaping the benefits from Web user growth. No longer will a simple ad randomly thrown at users or displayed for a few seconds on a computer screen suffice.

It is the goal for RD to set a new standard, recognizing that understanding the Internet consumer through obtaining direct feedback while constantly and instantaneously measuring their habits is becoming a necessity to all Internet marketers.

The market for user incentives can be broken down into two major segments. The first is the free Internet access market, where NetZero, Spinway, and 1stUp are the three major competitors. The market for free internet access was expected to grow from 1.5 million users in 2000 to just under 10 million in 2004, although the prediction is already being outpaced.

MARKET COMPETITORS

The two market leaders who are competing most intensely to set the standard in Web traffic analysis and metrics are (1) NetRatings/Neilsons and (2) Media Metrix. Media Metrix, with annual sales over $20 million, has the advantage of being one of the first movers in this market. Meanwhile, the newcomer NetRatings has netted annual sales of some $3 million. The two companies derive their statistics from control audiences. The Media Metrix control audience is 50,000. NetRatings has 35,000. Like the industry for Internet marketing intelligence, these two relatively young companies came forth with innovative ideas and acted on them. Though there are definitely areas where both Media Metrix and NetRatings can improve, they have reached a new frontier in the Internet industry.

PC Data Online is another competitor in Web traffic analysis. The company launched a Web traffic software package in April 1999, and the most recent research reports it has 100,000 volunteers signed onto the service. This base allows the company to charge $9,500 a year to any business interested in the information the volunteers are able to provide. The progress of PC Data Online as a major competitor is as yet somewhat inconclusive. Only time will tell what their role within the industry will be.

The market leader in Internet site-centric Web traffic analysis is Hitbox.com. This company places its own proprietary software on business client Web sites, but only has the capability to understand and breakdown through analysis the client's own Web site traffic. R-Data not only understands users, but can also contact them in real-time to see where they are going while they surf the Internet. RD can have a real-time focus group meeting via a chat room and through instant messaging.

STRATEGY SUMMARY

Following is how RD plans to implement its strategy.

FLEXIBLE USER REWARD SYSTEM

At the heart of R-Data's reward system is a point-based incentive program. Users will accrue reward points for interacting with RD that will be applied towards goods and services such as free Internet access, or monetary rewards. Pay-as-you-surf companies have not built in revenue streams to support free Internet services and cannot easily do so without putting themselves at significant financial risk. Free Internet access companies lock users into a single reward/incentive. Because these services are almost completely funded through ad banners, the service can be frustrating to users, who must either sacrifice screen space or constantly interact with the software console provided by the ISP, on penalty of having service shut down.

R-Data, on the other hand, has an innovative new technology that has the potential of increasing its revenues by 20 percent with little to no user interaction. We call it "Real Time Data Collection" and "Real Time Market Interaction." Given this flexibility in revenue stream, we can allow users to quickly "earn" or pay for the Internet access with trivial amounts of interaction with RD (one or two surveys per month). Users will receive additional prizes with more interaction or can minimize the ad banner portion of RD screens for the remainder of the month. Currently, we are negotiating with strategic partners so accumulated points can earn a free CD that month, a software package, credit card payments, or a variety of other popular incentives.

According to International Data Corp., the number of broadband users alone will grow from 2.4 million in 1999 to 14.7 million users in 2004—an increase from 5.5 percent of the total U.S. Internet access market to 21.9 percent. With our business model, we can quickly provide incentives to move into this market for both corporate partners and users. Businesses that are not currently interested in free Internet access companies include broadband service providers, cellular phone companies, premium content providers, and any other industry interested in having the prices of their products and services reduced by RD's point system. When a company partners with R-Data, they can easily apply the reward points that users earn toward the cost of these services.

OPPORTUNITIES AND BENCHMARKS

Companies in both our target industries have shown that they are able to compete successfully in a public offering. In September 1999 NetZero, the leader in free Internet access, raised $170 million. In May 1999, Media Metrix, the market leader in Internet Web traffic measurement, completed a public offering that raised $50 million. Because these companies rushed to market so early, they have made many mistakes that RData can capitalize on. Having thoroughly researched their business models, we have come up with solid improvements that give our company the potential for greater success and allow us to competitively address this rapidly expanding industry while still providing enough time to formulate a robust business model and product.

UNMATCHED SERVICES

The R-Data console was designed to attract and maintain a large Internet user base, supported by special features that promote a sense of community and usefulness. RD features that are not associated with many of our competitors include an embedded media player, chat client, instant messaging list, survey indicator, and site review.

LARGE USER BASE

A distinct disadvantage for our competitors, such as Media Metrix and NetRatings, is the number of their users. They do not have enough users on which to base an accurate report of Internet usage. When there are more than 11 million Web sites, it is not realistic to expect that 34,000 users can effectively report on very many of them. Using the marketing techniques previously discussed, R-Data plans to address this problem by reaching a large enough user base (on the scale of Net Zero's 3 million users) to accurately represent the Internet population.

LOWER CUSTOMER ACQUISITION/RETENTION COST

The average cost of acquiring new customers is defined as the marketing budget divided by the total number of new users. This cost does not, however, cover the cost of retaining customers after winning them over. Costs for customer acquisition range from $33 for Amazon.com to $3,000 for TheStreet.com.

Additional research has made it possible to estimate the cost of customer service. The cost for a live agent managing a customer desk is $33.00, chat room-based customer service is $7.80, and a purchase-based customer agent is $1.17. Our licensing fee for the cobranded RD will be in the range of a few dollars a month and should do more to facilitate acquiring and keeping a customer than a traditional marketing campaign. It will allow businesses to interact with their customers via chat rooms very cost-effectively, and it should encourage users to sign up their friends, increasing the likelihood of additional users becoming customers.

PRO FORMA FINANCIAL STATEMENTS

R-Data
Pro-Forma Balance Sheet: 2003-2007 *(in thousands)*

	Year 01	Year 02	Year 03	Year 04	Year 05
Assets					
Current Assets					
Cash and cash equivalents	$4,239	$8,499	$15,500	$40,356	$66,300
Fixed Assets					
Software	21	42	85	171	342
Computer equipment	59	47	96	148	211
Network equipment	3	5	11	22	44
Office equipment	1	19	39	79	158
Furniture and fixtures	9	3	6	13	26
Less: Accumulated depreciation	(10)	(21)	(42)	(85)	(171)
Total fixed assets	83	95	195	348	610
TOTAL ASSETS	**4,322**	**8,594**	**15,695**	**40,704**	**66,910**

Liabilities and equity

Accounts payable	10	20			
Computer leases	23	36	66	141	292
TOTAL LIABILITIES	33	56	66	141	292

Owners' Equity

Preferred stock	8	8	8	8	8
Additional paid in capital	8,180	28,180	28,180	28,180	28,180
Retained earnings/(loss)	(3,899)	(19,650)	(12,559)	12,375	38,430
TOTAL EQUITY	4,289	8,538	15,629	40,563	66,618
TOTAL LIABILITIES AND EQUITY	4,322	8,594	15,695	40,704	66,910

R-Data
Pro Forma Income Statement: 2003–2007

	Year 01	Year 02	Year 03	Year 04	Year 05
Sales					
Gross sales	$20,368	$87,003	$129,801	$161,617	$398,591
Cost of goods sold					
User incentives/rewards	27,168	66,937	85,837	104,737	284,681
GROSS MARGIN	(6,800)	20,066	43,964	56,880	113,910
Operating Expenses					
Advertising	5,492	5,850	7,500	14,365	33,208
Charitable contributions	-	522	1,318	1,403	3,245
Bank service charges	2	5	7	10	25
Delivery	3	7	10	16	37
Health insurance	72	144	216	324	756
General insurance	36	72	108	162	378
Professional fees	24	48	72	108	252
Rent	96	192	288	432	1,008
DSL/Frame relay	30	60	90	135	315
Supplies	7	14	21	32	75
Utilities	24	48	72	108	252
Leases, computer	18	36	54	81	189
Travel	84	168	252	378	882
Conferences	18	36	54	81	189
Maintenance	4	8	12	19	44
Payroll	2,506	4,992	7,488	11,232	26,217
Payroll taxes	350	698	1,048	1,572	3,670
Depreciation	9	18	27	41	95
Patent legal expense	24	48	72	108	252
TOTAL EXPENSES	8,799	12,966	18,709	30,607	71,089
NET INCOME/(LOSS)	(15,599)	7,100	25,255	26,273	42,821

COMPANY SERVICE COMPARISON

COMPANY		USER INCENTIVES			INCOME SOURCES					MARKETING INFORMATION			
Symbol	Company	Free ISP	User Rewards	User Chat	Ad Banner	Monthly Access Fee	Real Time Surveys	Real Time Data	Licensing Fee	Real Time Competitor	Real Time Interaction	Uses Cookie	Real Time Demo Data
-	R-Data	Yes	Yes	Yes	Yes	No	Yes	Yes	Yes	Yes	Yes	No	Yes
NZRO	Net.Zero	Yes	No	No	Yes	No	No	N/A	No	N/A	No	No	N/A
AOL	AOL	No	No	Yes	Yes	$22	No	N/A	No	N/A	No	Yes	N/A
ELNK	Earthlink	No	No	No	No	$20	No	No	No	No	No	Yes	No
-	Spinway	Yes	No	Yes	Yes	No	No	N/A	Yes	Yes	No	No	Yes
-	1st Up	Yes	No	N/A	Yes	No	N/A	N/A	Yes	N/A	No	No	N/A
AADV	All Advantage	No	Yes	No	Yes	No	N/A	Yes	No	N/A	No	No	N/A
MMXI	Media Matrix	No	No	No	N/A	No	N/A	Yes	No	N/A	N/A	No	Yes
NTRT	Net Ratings	No	No	No	N/A	No	N/A	Yes	No	N/A	N/A	No	Yes
DCLK	Double Click	No	No	No	Yes	No	No	No	No	No	No	Yes	No
TFSM	24/7 Media	No	No	No	Yes	No	No	No	No	No	No	Yes	No

FINANCIAL COMPARISONS

Symbol	Company	Industry	Launch Date	IPO Date	# Users (millions)	Price/ Month	Market Cap	Quarterly Revenues	Quarterly Net (Loss)	Percent Growth
-	R-Data	ISP/Market	-	-	N/A	$0	N/A	N/A	N/A	N/A
-	J Link	ISP/Market	-	-	N/A	$0	N/A	$6.0 M	($4.0 M)	N/A
NZRO	Net Zero	ISP/Market	1998	1999	3 M	$0	$3.7 B	$7.7 M	($14.9M)	-27%
AOL	AOL	ISP	1985	1992	20 M	$20	$140.0 B	$1.5 B	N/A	N/A
ELNK	Earthlink	ISP	1994	1997	1.6 M	$20	N/A	$90.0 M	($35.0 M)	N/A
-	Spinway	ISP/Market	1999	-	N/A	$0	N/A	N/A	N/A	N/A
-	1st Up	ISP/Market	1999	-	1 M	$0	N/A	N/A	N/A	N/A
AADV	All Advantage	Rewards	1999	-	5 M	$0	N/A	N/A	N/A	N/A

COMPARISON OF THE INTERNET MARKET RESEARCH INDUSTRY

Symbol	Company	Industry	Launch Date	IPO Date	# Users (millions)	# Ad. Imp.	Price/ Ad ($)	Market Cap.	Quarterly Revenue	Quarterly Net (Loss)	Percent Growth
-	R-Data	ISP/Market	-	-	N/A	N/A	-	N/A	N/A	N/A	N/A
-	J Link	ISP/Market	-	-	-	-	-	N/A	-	($4.0 M)	N/A
MMXI	Media Matrix	Web Measure	1997	1999	$0.05 M	$0.5 M	N/A	$0.7 B	$5.5 M	($2.6 M)	-18%
NTRT	NetRatings	Web Measure	1998	1999	$0.04 M	N/A	N/A	$1.2 B	$0.5 M	($3.6 M)	N/A
DCLK	Double Click	Ad Network	1996	1998	N/A	$17 B	0.50-0.83	$8.8 B	$45.0 M	($5.3 M)	2098%
TFSM	24/7 Media	Ad Network	1998	1998	N/A	$2.5 B	0.33-0.67	$1.4 B	$24.3 M	($11.7 M)	213%

CHAPTER 10

CRITICAL SUCCESS FACTORS

"If you fail to plan, you plan to fail"
-Unknown Author

No quotation could be more accurate when a company is thinking about going public. A common mistake of many companies is to rush into their IPO. The following are some of the critical factors that distinguish highly successful companies. How does your company measure up?

- *Successful companies outperformed the competition before, during, and after the IPO.* Critical to the successful IPO is the competitive position of the company at the time of the offering. The stronger the firm was before the IPO, the more successful it tends to be after. The risks of going public are higher for those that are less competitive at the start of the process.

  Companies that were highly successful were significantly stronger than their public competitors gauged by all criteria, financial and nonfinancial. As a result, highly successful companies went public with share prices that averaged 20 percent higher than less successful companies (Spiess and Pettway, 1997). Companies that had the most successful IPOs had an average-market value that was significantly greater than the market value of less successful companies, and over time this market value difference significantly increased.

• *Successful companies began the transformation to a public company months or years before the actual IPO*. The IPO was viewed as a process rather than an event by companies that were successful. Early in the process, they introduced new systems and approaches, implemented strong communication programs, and executed strategic transactions. Many companies increased their success by initiating employee incentive programs, which have proved to have greater significance in the long run than any other policy changes companies implement. Distinguished by improvements in planning, financial accounting and reporting, internal controls, executive committees, and investor relations policies, the highly successful companies set themselves advantageously apart from the others.

The companies with the greatest success in their offerings reportedly reevaluated their plans for such projects as recapitalizations, acquisitions, and other financings immediately before or after the IPO.

The earlier the change initiatives were put in place, the more likely the success of the IPO. Conversely, companies that launched change initiative programs less than a year before an IPO were less likely to achieve the desired result of a successful publicly held company.

• *Successful companies applied the Balanced Scorecard approach*. The more successful the IPO, the higher the company ranked on such nonfinancial measures as the credibility and the quality of management, customer service, retention of employees, and strength of the corporate culture, all the elements of the Balanced Scorecard. They also tended to be ahead of competitors in building a winning team, installing an information-based infrastructure, and drawing on the advice of objective business advisors. Analysts and investors notice these sorts of things.

FORM A "DREAM TEAM"

As it works through the process of transformation into a public company, a company's success depends heavily on a coordinated team effort.

Typically, a winning team consists of three major groups (1) talented executives and employees, (2) a strong board of directors, and (3) experienced external advisors. A high-impact team will help the company design and execute the right business strategies and will provide invaluable expertise during the IPO process.

The time to form a winning team is not three or four months before the public offering. The team needs to be functioning efficiently as far ahead of the IPO as possible. The first leadership challenge in forming a winning team is to assess the company's current situation and consider whether additions or other changes need to be made both in the composition of the team and in how the company rewards some of its members. For example, the company might consider upgrading its executive compensation program, augmenting the board of directors, and establishing positive relationships with underwriters and other investor groups.

The first segment part of the dream team that deserves attention is the internal team, the company's executives and their role in the IPO process. Our examination of this area will include a discussion of the critical issue of an effective executive compensation program. We will then move on to selection and compensation of board members, the structure of the board, and how to get the most out of the board. Finally, we will talk about choosing and managing members of the advisory team, underwriters, auditors, lawyers, and investor relations firms.

THE INTERNAL TEAM

The inner circle, the company's executive management team, should be one of the company's most valuable assets. The company will depend on them all through the IPO process as well as during the strategic initiatives that precede going public.

Management represents the company to the financial community. It has been found (Miller and Reilly, 1997) that the nonfinancial criteria of the Balanced Scorecard, such as the quality of management and the ability to attract and retain talented people, constitute 35 percent of an institutional investor's decision. Underwriters and investors will be closely assessing the strength of the company's management team.

THE EXECUTIVE MANAGEMENT TEAM

Tremendous demands will be made on executive time before, during, and after the public offering. The people running the company must not only be prepared to accept these responsibilities, they must be capable of completing them successfully. Before the company embarks on the IPO, it will want to assess its current management team. Do they have the breadth and depth of knowledge the company needs to achieve both short-term and long-term success as a public company? Consider critical skills, character requirements, and experience needed for the ideal team and look for gaps that need to be filled. For instance, when contemplating a public offering, the chief executive officer (CEO) will often hire a chief financial officer (CFO) who has had experience in dealing with the demands on a public company.

The difference between the top-performing and the average company depends increasingly on the blend of skills at the highest levels. Companies of today are guided less by a single individual than by a balanced management team, another aspect of the Balanced Scorecard to keep the company in check. At the very top of a successful company there are likely to be two people (1) a CEO and (2) a CFO or a chief operating officer (COO). Their traits should be different but complementary. They play very different roles.

The CEO's chief concern will be the company's relationships with the entire array of external stakeholders both before and after the IPO. He or she must be a confident, outgoing leader and an enthusiastic spokesperson for the company, someone who can bond especially with the various new stakeholders. The CFO or COO will be more concerned with running the business and achieving the best possible performance. This person must be experienced and comfortable with the demands of responsible accounting and information systems.

These two leaders will spend a great deal of time on the road, particularly during major transactions like an IPO process. It is therefore imperative that the company also have in place another level of management, a layer of competent people who can independently manage such operations as production, sales and marketing, finance (controller), and management information systems (MIS). Some of these positions may have to be filled by outsiders and integrated into the company.

The 1990s was the decade of the management team. It is not clear how this trend will plan out in future years, but it is clear that management teams have been able to bring together fragmented companies, and by making them more efficient and productive, these teams are serving shareholders well.

COMPENSATION OF THE MANAGEMENT TEAM

To attract and retain a strong management team, the company must offer a competitive and comprehensive compensation plan. Because the market for talented executives is extremely tight today, having the right compensation program is particularly important. Putting in place a competitive compensation program is much more challenging for private companies because they cannot offer publicly traded stock, the form of compensation that has been most emphasized in the past 10 years.

Two powerful new elements in compensation plans of public companies are (1) outright stock grants (non-qualified stock grants) and (2) stock options (incentive stock options). The pre-IPO company has a unique opportunity. Because of the jump in stock value that can be expected from an IPO, the perceived value of the company's stock may never be greater. Therefore, used carefully, a company's stock may become the most powerful compensation mechanism for attracting and retaining key employees, thus in turn enhancing company and shareholder value.

Before an IPO, 75 percent of the companies in a recent research survey had improved their executive compensation programs. This is a high-payoff undertaking. Analysts and investors pay considerable attention to the strategic aspects of compensation because it can improve the company's ability to attract and retain talented people while ensuring that compensation is aligned with shareholder interests. Even if the company already has an effective compensation program, it should be reexamined as the company prepares for the IPO and the company would be well advised to use stock-based compensation to its advantage. However, it must also consider potential dilution impact, comparable to the concept of a "smaller piece of a bigger pie."

The compensation program should be approached like any other major business investment, with the goal of maximizing the company's return on investment. Compensation planning demands careful and informed consideration of shareholder value, accounting rules, tax laws, leading-edge compensation practices, and much more. Many costly errors can be avoided by consulting respected compensation consultants.

Normally, for a public company, compensation decisions are in a public arena, under the guidance of a compensation committee. In this new environment, the company will need to communicate its pay policies not only to employees but also to stock exchange officials, regulators, investors and the public at large. The compensation committee, part of the board of directors, will assume greater responsibility for designing and monitoring the company's compensation practices.

Preferably, a company that plans to go public should reserve a pool of stock to be used for compensation in advance. The pool should contain enough stock to cover all pre-IPO option grants plus all expected incentives for two or three years after the IPO. Authorizing the grants in advance sends a clear message internally and externally. It helps the company manage employee expectations while giving investors the information they need to make decisions about the potential dilution impact of shares used for compensation. Planning in advance also eliminates the need to obtain shareholder approval to reserve additional shares for compensation programs shortly after the IPO.

The compensation plan is a living process. It requires continual monitoring periodic updating as the company grows and as regulations and best practices evolve. Starting from an articulated compensation philosophy as a foundation, the company should continuously ask whether compensation packages that are currently in place are competitive enough to attract and retain the quality of executive desired.

BOARD OF DIRECTORS

Long before the IPO actually happens, the board of directors should play a key role in policy decisions. The board consists of individuals elected by the corporation shareholders to oversee management of the corporation. Members of the board may be paid in cash, stock or both. They meet several times each year and have legal responsibility for corporate activities.

The composition of the board is important to investors who are evaluating the company. To the boards of both private and public companies, outside directors (people who are not management and major share-holders) bring specialized expertise and an independent perspective. The company should consider inviting individuals with proven expertise within their specialized industries to serve as directors. For example, executives of other companies may bring operations expertise. Bankers may be able to provide financial advice; lawyers, accountants, and other professionals could bring their specialized expertise; and academics might be invited for their knowledge of technical or operational matters.

Outside board members not only enhance credibility with the investment community but can help strengthen management of the company. Strong and respected outsiders can be especially valuable advocates if the company encounters a rough period after the IPO. If the company's aim is to have its stock listed on a national exchange like the New York or American Stock Exchange or on the National Association of Securities Dealers and Automated Quotations (Nasdaq) Stock Market, the company will have to comply with the corporate governance requirements of that exchange, which usually include requirements for certain numbers of independent directors.

Companies going public often try to identify as candidates for directors individuals with strong reputations within their industry, in public service, or in other areas of public life. However, when they only have limited familiarity with the company such individuals are sometimes reluctant to assume the director role due to the liability they must legally assume.

The Sarbanes-Oxley Act of 2002 has further complicated matters. The act sets up a national the Public Company Accounting Oversight Board. Board responsibilities under the act, include:

• To set its budget and manage operations.

• Inspect and register public accounting firms (registered firms) that prepare audit reports for issuers.

• Establish, adopt, or modify auditing, quality control, ethics, independence, and other standards for public company audits.

• Enforce compliance with the Act, the rules of the Board, professional standards, and the securities laws relating to the preparation and issuance of audit reports and related obligations and liabilities of auditors.

- Investigate registered firms for potential violations of applicable rules relating to audits.

- Impose sanctions for violations.

- Perform such other duties or functions as the Board or Commission determines necessary.

The Board will have five financially literate members, each serving full-time and appointed for a five-year term. Two of the members must be or have been certified public accountants (CPAs). The other three may not ever have been CPAs. The chair may be one of the CPA members only if that person has not been a practicing CPA for five years. No member, may concurrent with service on the Board, "share in any of the profits of, or receive payments from, a public accounting firm" other than "fixed continuing payments," such as retirement payments.

Under the Securities Act of 1933, a member of a company board can be held liable if a registration statement contains any untrue statement of a material fact or fails to state a material fact that was required. As today's boards face the growing risk of litigation, companies are finding new ways to give their directors legal protection. Although the SEC historically has not favored indemnification for securities law violations, the vast majority of public companies do buy D&O insurance for directors and most have amended their corporate charters to permit indemnification of directors. If this were not the case, public companies would be hard pressed environment to find qualified people willing to serve as directors.

BOARD SIZE

In general, a larger board should provide greater expertise and wealth of experience than a smaller board, but this must be weighed against the disadvantage that a larger group may be less cooperative than a smaller board in judging some aspects of company's business and therefore may not be able to function as effectively.

The size of boards of directors varies according to numerous factors, industry group, asset size, and sales volume. According to the American Bar Association's *Corporate Director's Guidebook*, complex corporations tend to have larger boards, averaging about 15 members, while smaller industrial concerns average 8 to 9 members. Corporations that have larger boards tend to operate in committees, which are more manageable.

In ascertaining the appropriate number of board members, many companies look to the kinds of issues that either require or would benefit from board involvement, the complexity of the company's operations, the size of boards elsewhere in the industry, and the cost of obtaining and retaining highly qualified board members.

BOARD TERMS

Currently, there are no laws that dictate the length of time board members may serve. Nor are companies regulated in terms of frequency of reelection or replacement of board members. In the fallout from current accounting messes, however, it will probably be only a matter of time before this changes.

With the expectation that there will be minimal turnover, some companies elect their entire board annually. Other companies establish longer terms for board members, usually three to five years, and stagger the elections so that only a small percentage of the board stand for election in any year. This is common when a company is concerned both with board continuity and protection against unsolicited offers. Some have a mandatory retirement age for board members and some have rules on the maximum number of terms a member may serve.

BOARD RESPONSIBILITIES

The basic responsibility of a corporate director is to enhance the interests of the corporation. A director demonstrates responsibility by performing his or her duties for the company in a way that can best be described as trustworthy and conscientious. While that idea may seem obvious, it is important that directors fully comprehend the far-reaching impact of such fundamental responsibilities. Failure to comprehend these responsibilities can lead to liability for the corporation and the director.

Conscientious refers to acting in good faith, in a way believed to be in the best interests of the corporation, and with the care that a prudent person in a similar situation would exercise. Conscientious behavior has numerous important attributes, such as consistently attending board meetings and taking the time before a meeting to become fully informed by reviewing all the information, financial and otherwise, that is needed to make an informed decision. By doing this type of homework in advance, the director can ascertain whether he or she feels comfortable relying on the reports of, say, independent accountants or the corporation's legal counsel.

Trustworthy refers to whether the director is performing his or her duties in the interest of the corporation's shareholders, not in the interest of another organization or person or in the director's own interest. Directors should be constantly alert for anything issue that might be construed as conflicting with the best interests of the corporation and generally should excuse themselves from voting on matters that could be interpreted as presenting a conflict of interest. The Sarbanes-Oxley act has placed a much heavier burden on directors to keep the best interests of the company always at the forefront of their actions.

Directors are responsible to shareholders because their primary role is overseeing the activities of management. Once an IPO is completed, the company will have a significant continuing responsibility to its new shareholders.

INDEPENDENT DIRECTORS IN FACT AND IN APPEARANCE

The board of directors of a public company, or one that is about to go public, should be organized to function as an independent evaluator and observer of the company's performance and affairs.

The composition of the board will be a major factor in determining the group's effectiveness and efficiency in promoting the objectives of the corporation. Boards are usually comprised of both independent directors and management. A *management director* is normally a senior executive of the corporation, someone whose primary duty is as an employee. Although these members are of extreme importance due to their expertise in managing the company and their day-to-day familiarity with its operations, an increasing number of board members are now independent directors.

All publicly traded companies must have independent directors. Independent directors are valued because they can be more her objective about the company's dealings. The investment community prefers to see boards comprised of members who do not simply accept the recommendations of management. Such a board will be a strength as the company ventures forward in the IPO process.

BOARD COMMITTEES

In the committee structure, numerous public companies have found an efficient effective way for their boards to function successfully. This structure is especially useful for outside directors who have extensive commitments elsewhere. The committee structure also allows independent directors to specialize. The company thus cultivates a greater knowledge base about specific areas, from financial reporting and internal financial controls to management selection and compensation.

The majority of directors on most committees are independent members. The size and number of the board committees vary by industry group as well as company. Like the board itself, the primary advantage of large committees is the broader experience base represented by the members. The disadvantage is that larger committees may become difficult to manage, hard for the chairperson to keep focused. Each company must determine the appropriate size for its unique situation. Some of the more common committees are discussed below.

THE AUDIT COMMITTEE

The audit committee has numerous tasks, among them oversight of the financial reporting process and review of the work of both internal and independent auditors. To perform its function effectively, the audit committee must understand the company's business, the industry and its inherent risks, and the financial reporting process itself. The audit committee will be helped in its oversight duties by maintaining open communication with both internal auditors and the company's independent auditing firm. Of utmost importance to the audit committee's success is effective communication of the committee with management, the full board, the internal auditors, and the independent auditors.

The audit committee is the most common board committee. It was first recommended by the New York Stock Exchange (NYSE) in 1939. Today the NYSE, the American Stock Exchange (AMEX), and Nasdaq all require companies listed on their exchange to have audit committees. The AMEX and Nasdaq require that a majority of the members be independent, but the NYSE requires the committee to be comprised entirely of independent directors.

The size of audit committees will vary from company to company. However, the Treadway Commission suggests there be at least three members, and each member should be an active participant in committee activities. Between three and five members is fairly standard for most companies (Field, 1997).

Though the duties of an audit committee may be relatively similar from company to company, its methods of operation and style need not be. Rather, the operational method and styles should be closely tailored to the objectives, requirements, and circumstances of the organization the committee is designed to serve. The background and expertise of directors as well as their depth of knowledge of the company's financial position should determine the nature and scope of an audit committee's activities. Some industries, such as banking, have specialized regulatory requirements that also play a major role in the committee's duties.

Typically, the audit committee is set up through a formal board resolution. The audit committee's oversight responsibilities must be distinguished from any involvement it has in day-to-day management of the company. The committee must not be considered an adversary of management. Rather, it is part of the corporation's governance process.

Audit committee charters typically require that only outside directors be members and most research studies (Field, 1997) and regulatory agencies have encouraged this practice. Most important, members must be committed to the undertaking and have adequate time to devote to the committee's work.

The role of audit committees has been the subject of heightened interest in the financial community for the past several years due to the numerous gross negligence suits being brought against companies for misleading financial statements. The NYSE and the National Association of Securities Dealers (NASD) sponsored the Blue Ribbon Committee on Improving the Effectiveness of Corporate Audit Committees (the Blue Ribbon Committee), charging it to formulate recommendations on how to empower audit committees to function as the ultimate "guardian of investor interests and corporate accountability" (Jenkinson, 2001). The Blue Ribbon Committee's February 1999 report contained a series of recommendations for the securities exchanges, the SEC, and the American Institute of Certified Public Accountants (AICPA) aimed at improving the effectiveness of audit committees. However, prior to any of the Blue Ribbon Committee's recommendations become regulations or rules, the SEC, the securities exchanges, and the AICPA's Auditing Standards Board must act on them.

COMPENSATION COMMITTEE

The compensation committee reviews salary progression, bonus allocations, stock options and awards, and the award of supplemental benefits and perquisites for key executives, comparing them to the company's compensation objectives as well as the overall performance of the company. In general, the compensation committee is primarily concerned with compensation for senior executives. If it is to be an effective tool for corporate planning on behalf of the shareholders, the committee should be composed solely of independent directors.

Recently, executive compensation has become one the most hotly debated issues of corporate governance. At the center of the debates is the question of whether the substantial lucrative salary and benefits packages for the CEO and other senior executives are justified by their performance and the performance of the corporation. A privately held company need not disclose compensation of key executives, but public companies must reveal the compensation of its CEO and its next four most highly compensated executives. A responsible compensation committee of the board of directors can help the board evaluate the performance of these officers and decide whether the compensation is justified.

From a strategic viewpoint, the compensation committee should ascertain how to achieve the goals and objectives of the corporation through adoption of an appropriate compensation philosophy and an effective compensation program. This is of extreme importance for a company about to go public because compensation is such an important factor in attracting and retaining management talent best suited for the company.

The compensation committee may seek assistance from outside compensation consultants, just as the audit committee has access to outside advisors. Specialists can advise the committee about how competitive the company's compensation structure is within the industry and in comparison with companies of similar size in other industries.

EXECUTIVE COMMITTEE

Between board meetings, the executive committee can serve as a primary link between the board and management. The committee is usually granted a wide range of powers to ensure that important matters that cannot wait until the next scheduled board meeting receive timely attention. Executive committees can also help boards function more efficiently. In particular, when the board is large, the committee may serve as a sounding board for general management problems that affect the corporation as a whole.

Because of the invaluable wealth of knowledge and experience, a retired CEO or other senior executive may bring to the company, such people are often asked to serve on the executive committee. Often, chairs of other key board committees are also members of the executive committee. It is not surprising to find a larger percentage of management directors sitting on the executive committee, given its orientation toward management issues (Stoughton and Zechner, 1998).

FINANCE COMMITTEE

In times of active mergers and acquisitions and general financial uncertainty, the finance committee's role is more critical, particularly in larger companies. This committee is most likely to be found in larger corporations with complex financial structures.

The broad responsibility of the finance committee is financial decisions and planning. Among its responsibilities are to:

- Evaluate the financial information it receives and decide whether any plan of action is required.

- Stay abreast of the financial situation of the company.

- Advise management and the board on financial matters of concern.

Although usually not empowered to act on its own, the finance committee is sometimes authorized to make decisions on behalf of the full board between board meetings.

NOMINATING COMMITTEE

The job of the nominating committee has become ever more critical. With the Sarbanes-Oxley Act, it has become increasingly difficult for corporate America to find qualified candidates willing to serve on boards of directors. This committee is given the responsibility of identifying and thoroughly screening candidates for initial board positions or board vacancies. To do this, the nominating committee must consider the broader issues of the composition and the organization of the board, including committee assignments. The nominating committee evaluates the board itself and its members and reviews the company's management succession planning to ensure proper transitions.

Candidates recommended to the nominating committee for board membership are often people who have had prior contact with the company's management team and other board members. Increasingly, however, nominating committees are relying on the help of outside consultants to locate good candidates. The outside consultants generally help screen candidates to provide greater assurance that the candidates are independent in both fact and appearance.

In general, all nominees recommended by the committee stand for election by the shareholders. However, some nominating committees have granted the authority to elect a director to fill a vacancy for the remainder of a term.

WORKING EFFECTIVELY WITH THE BOARD

A strong relationship between management and the board of directors is more important today than ever before. Two separate trends best illustrate this point:

1. An unstable business environment increases the need for a cooperative relationship. The pressures typically faced today range from consolidations and downsizings to international competition, economic turmoil, and constantly accelerating change. If top management and the board work as a team, they can more easily meet challenges as they occur. Together they can create and sustain a strong business strategy and adapt quickly when changes need to be made.

2. Boards have lately become much more active in overseeing all aspects of company operations. An active board can be an asset to the company. Companies with active boards generally perform better. *Business Week's* "best 25 boards" far outpaced the Standard & Poor's (S&P) 500 in 2002, producing annual shareholder returns of 25.4 percent compared with an S&P average of 17.9 percent *(Business Week,* December 12, 2002, pp. 71–82). Conversely boards, that have little power and low involvement have been associated with poor financial performance.

The management team can do much to make the board part of the forecasts for success set forth by the company, even in the worst-case scenario of an unsympathetic or an uncaring board. The company can encourage the board to participate in strategic planning, explicitly define directors' responsibilities, keep the board thoroughly informed, and communicate in a timely, accurate, and honest way.

ENCOURAGE INPUT FROM THE BOARD

Board support of the company's strategic plan is a corporate-governance imperative. A recent survey concluded that boards spend an average of one-fourth of their time on corporate strategy (Jenkinson and Ljungquist, 2001). While it is ultimately management's job to create and implement a winning strategy, the strategy should either be created together with the board or be approved by the board.

If company management is new and the board is inherited, the new management must make every effort to understand the board's goals for the organization. The better management understands the board's agenda, the easier it will be to draft and implement a strategic plan that is endorsed by the board.

DEFINE RESPONSIBILITIES EXPLICITLY

The division of responsibility between board and management must be clear and explicitly stated. Especially where the board is inherited or unsympathetic, explicit job descriptions for directors and company management are advisable.

Clear expectations of criteria for measuring management effectiveness will help to eliminate sources of conflict before they arise. Ideally, management should set performance goals in conjunction with the board. At minimum, all parties should agree on annual performance goals for the company. In turn, management should establish criteria to evaluate itself and the performance of its members. The best boards conduct both self-evaluations and peer reviews (Jenkinson and Ljungqvist, 2001).

KEEP THE BOARD COMPLETELY INFORMED

A critical task for the management team is to ensure that the board is informed about market trends and company progress. It is particularly importance to share negative information with the board. Unpleasant surprises will undermine board trust. Unfortunately, in today's economic climate, corporate whistle blowing of improper financial reporting or other problems has become a moral imperative for everyone associated with the company.

It is best if the information flows both ways. Just as management can provide information to the board, a strong board can often contribute knowledge to the company, along with access to the directors' network of business and personal relationships.

KEEP COMMUNICATIONS TIMELY, ACCURATE, AND HONEST

The purpose of communication with the board is to gain credibility and support in creating and implementing company strategy. If communication is good, strategic initiatives can become cooperative ventures involving management and board, with the board taking an advisory role in major company decisions. Such a cooperative relationship will allow management and the board to maintain a shared focus of the company's goals.

Timely communication with the board will prevent misunderstandings and uncertainties. To facilitate good communication, management must be available on a regular basis to respond to the board's concerns. Lack of responsiveness is likely to generate concern and distrust among board members. Regular meetings will keep the board informed and the board will be able to give management feedback on how they perceive performance as compared to the overall strategic plan.

To summarize, the best relationship between company management and the board is one of mutual respect, cooperation, and shared responsibility. Management should communicate regularly and honestly with board members, should remain accessible, and should encourage open discussion of all major company concerns.

THE COMPANY'S EXTERNAL ADVISORY TEAM

If a company's outside directors are chosen well, they will add to the sophistication and quality of the company's winning team. Of equal importance is the selection of professional advisors. The underwriters, for instance, will be absolutely critical to the success of the IPO because they will help the company present itself effectively to investors and will ultimately sell the securities. The company also will need a law firm that has substantial SEC experience and an accounting firm that fully understands all the complexities involved in taking a company public.

The quality of the external advisory team can make an enormous impact on the ultimate success or failure of an IPO. The most successful companies retain close relationships with these professionals, keeping communication with them open and honest, in good times and bad (Jenkinson and Ljungqvist, 2001).

UNDERWRITERS

Few companies attempt to sell their own shares through a public offering without the assistance of underwriters, and for good reason. The underwriters syndicate has the distribution channels, the contacts, and the expertise to reach a much broader group of investors than any company could on its own. The syndicate will lend greater credibility to the offering. They will target those investors for whom the shares are likely to have the most investment appeal. The syndicate has both the resources to invest in this time-consuming effort and the expertise to avoid the potential negative consequences of an improperly handled selling attempt.

In addition to the initial sales effort, underwriters typically play a significant role in maintaining a strong and stable aftermarket for a company's securities. They serve as market makers, buying and selling shares on the interdealer market and in general, they help keep up interest in the company's shares among investors and analysts. Because the underwriting process is so critical, an entire chapter is devoted to the topic later in the book.

INDEPENDENT AUDITORS

The company will want to select an experienced independent auditor that has enough depth and breadth to serve as a trusted business advisor throughout the IPO and beyond. It is wise to choose a firm with a strong national reputation for the quality of its experience in securities offerings and in dealing with the SEC. A full-service accounting firm has the resources necessary to provide a full range of auditing, accounting, and tax advice.

ADVISORY ROLE

The company's auditors should become involved in the early stages of a public offering. They will help the company assess the relative advantages and disadvantages of going public. They can advise on alternative sources of financing and help investigate those alternatives. They should also be able to give advice on the corporate tax implications and ascertain tax planning strategies must be taken into consideration. They can also help assess and approach underwriters and advise on negotiating with them.

SEC REQUIREMENTS

Highly capable auditors will not only help avoid costly errors and delays in the registration process, they will provide the company with continuing counsel and assistance in dealing with SEC reporting and many of the other obligations of a public company.

The auditors have a particularly strong role to play in one of the most important aspects of the prospectus, the financial disclosure package. For an established private company, the historical audited financial statements and financial highlights are the evidence of the earnings record. The company may need to supplement or update its business plan to include current cash flow analyses, sensitivity studies, industry and competition studies, and marketing analyses. Auditors can help present the financial disclosure package clearly, concisely, and in accordance with SEC regulations. They also can anticipate SEC concerns that can be addressed before the initial filing.

One of the SEC's financial disclosure requirements is a summary of selected financial data for a period of five years (not required for small business issuers). Although the SEC requires audited financial statements for only three years, some underwriters prefer that all years listed in the table of selected financial data be audited. Moreover, many SEC interpretations of GAAP differ from those commonly understood by private companies and therefore require particular consideration when an IPO is prepared. These SEC interpretations can necessitate significant changes in how financial information is presented. This fact of public company life underscores the importance of establishing a relationship with a professional services firm and having annual audits performed well in advance of a public offering.

Auditors typically will provide comfort letters at the request of the company's underwriters, who will rely on the letters as part of their due diligence with respect to financial information in the prospectus and the registration statement. A good long-term working relationship with a professional services firm will not only facilitate the registration process but will also prove valuable as the company matures as a public company.

THE INVESTOR RELATIONS FIRM

Selling the company's shares and maintaining investor interest in the aftermarket is not dissimilar from selling products or services to customers, depending as both do on advertising, name recognition, and publicity, a product support system, and good distribution channels. Although the underwriting syndicate will provide the distribution channels, the company preparing for an IPO needs to create a corporate image as the foundation for a strong investor relations program.

A good investor relations firm can be of great value. Such firms know the institutional market and can help design the institutional road show and the disclosure strategy. Creating a corporate image takes time, so the company should start working with an investor relations firm well in advance of the IPO, especially given that the SEC imposes restrictions on any new forms of advertising or publicity in which the company may engage once the company starts the registration process by retaining an underwriter.

The first step in creating a public image is to a thorough self-evaluation of the company and its future. Ask questions about the company's potential geographic appeal. For instance, depending on the company's product and its geographic product market area, shares solid in an IPO might be limited to a regional market, or they might attract national or even international interest.

In what industry does the company operate? That could bear on the company's appeal to investors. Industries that investors find more attractive than others command a higher price-earnings ratio. If the business might be classified in more than one way, aim for the classification that would bring in the highest price-earnings ratio. Some companies with diverse product lines might be identified with only one of their better-known products. A good publicity campaign could create a broader image for the company.

CHAPTER 11

THE FOUNDATION
FOR AN IPO

At this point much of the groundwork has been done for a successful IPO. The company has defined what it takes to be successful in its endeavors, chartered the business strategy, prepared the business plan, and perhaps undertaken one or more strategic transactions. A winning team is in place. But will the interests of the company and the shareholders best be served by a public offering?

A common mistake companies make is to start rolling out an IPO before they are ready to meet the numerous demands of being a public company. Say the company has now progressed from the planning phase to the execution phase. It is moving toward the starting line of the IPO event. Before the actual event takes place, the company must pull all the pieces together and complete the many different items on the pre-IPO "to do" list.

Now is the time for the company to set its priorities for the critical months just before the IPO. The company is actually starting the process of becoming a public company. This phase will help ensure that when the company does become publicly financed, it will be successful, and will meet and exceed the expectations of the market.

During the months before an IPO event, successful companies consider the following questions:

- What operating, personnel, and transactional milestones have yet to be completed before the company is ready to move into the IPO?

- Does the company have a clear plan for using the proceeds of the IPO? Can that plan be communicated to investors and analysts clearly and concisely?

- Has the company completed its "corporate housekeeping"?

- Is the market ready for the IPO at this time?

The company responses to these questions are key factors in the final decision to take the company public. They can provide the resources for both the IPO and the performance of company shares in the aftermarket.

THE IMPROVEMENT AGENDA

This is the time to revalidate the company's decision to go public by implementing all the changes planned during the earliest stages of the IPO process. Is the company where it needs to be in order to move forward into an IPO? The company will want to review the goals, strategies, and initiatives already set forth and make sure all the building blocks are in place.

Perhaps the company planned to make three acquisitions to move the company from $50 million to $150 million in volume. Or the company may have decided to reengineer its inventory control systems to gain efficiency and credibility. Just going through the externals of a transaction or an improvement program does not guarantee that the company will reap the benefits. By this time in the IPO process, the company should have seen significant changes in the wake of acquisitions or improvements, although considerable uncertainty may also have been added.

To be sure, the company can integrate a new business and its people into the daily operations of the company is imperative. The company must also ensure that any new inventory (or any other) system actually operates as planned and achieves the objectives for it. A company that tries to go public without integrating new companies or systems will be unlikely to meet its earnings estimates.

Earnings estimates cannot be taken lightly. They can in fact prove fatal. If the estimates are not met or exceeded, investor confidence will be greatly shaken, which could cause long-term damage because it reflects poorly on the company's credibility.

This early step in the IPO process is an important opportunity to review preparation efforts and fill any gaps. The concern is to be sure that all the initiatives that propel the company to the threshold of the IPO have been successfully integrated and are adding value. The company must be secure enough in its future direction to feel confident of meeting earnings forecasts quarter after quarter.

THE INFORMATION SYSTEM

A public company is required to provide reliable and timely financial information to investors. If a company's management and accounting information systems are inadequate, the time to put them in first-class working order is well before an IPO. There are legal liabilities for reporting misleading or false information, not to mention the loss of investor confidence that is bound to happen if information is not timely and accurate.

THE SYSTEM OF INTERNAL CONTROL

Many companies recognize the importance of strong internal controls. An effective internal control structure can help a company achieve financial goals, prevent loss of resources, and be confident that its financial statements are reliable.

Companies considering an IPO need to take a close look at their system of internal controls and evaluate how effective it is. The importance of internal controls became particularly clear with the enactment of the Foreign Corrupt Practices Act of 1977 (FCPA). The FCPA was a direct result of a public scandal that revealed that more than 400 U.S. companies had secretly made kickbacks, bribes, or other questionable payments to foreign officials to obtain or to maintain business connections.

There are two major provisions to the FCPA. The first, the conduct provision, which affects all U.S. companies, makes it illegal for any U.S. business to pay or to authorize payment of anything of value to foreign officials to obtain or to maintain business relationships. Many companies now have written codes of conduct that address these issues.

The second major provision, which relates to accounting, applies only to companies that file reports with the SEC under the Securities Exchange Act of 1934, publicly traded companies. This accounting provision has two major requirements: (1) Registrants must maintain records, books, and accounts that accurately reflect the transactions of the registrant; (2) registrants must establish a system of internal controls adequate to meet the following four requirements:

1. The recorded accountability for assets is compared with assets at reasonable intervals, and appropriate action is taken to resolve any differences.

2. Transactions are executed in accordance with management authorization, general or specific.

3. Transactions are recorded in a way that permits preparation of financial statements in conformity with GAAP and accounts for assets

4. Access to assets is permitted only with management authorization.

Adhering to the FCPA is a responsibility of management, subject to SEC enforcement.

In addition to the FCPA, other compliance obligations are mounting. The SEC recently issued ten financial rules and four proposals relating to the Sarbanes-Oxley Act of 2002. Complying with the recent sweeping changes in U.S. securities laws is complex, and will continue to challenge executives and audit committee members of publicly traded companies in the immediate future.

THE CORPORATE IMAGE

Because creating a strong corporate image takes time, a company should get its campaign in gear well in advance of the public offering, not only to prepare the ground for the IPO but also to have a strong image in place when SEC restrictions on any new forms of advertising once the registration process has begun.

As we discussed in the previous chapter, the image-building process begins with a complete and comprehensive self-evaluation that takes into account where and how the company operates, the product mix, industry classification options, and how the company is currently perceived. The company may choose to do this internally or to call in an image consultant. Only when the company has a clear understanding of where its image is and where it wants to go can it settle on a specific plan for getting there.

POTENTIAL INVESTORS

One crucial early question is: What types of investors does the company wish to attract? There are obvious advantages to luring institutional investors because they control a large portion of America's investment capital, but often they often have technical investment restrictions relating to, for example, the number and the price of a company's shares on the market and its earnings history, dividend policy, and stock exchange listing. These restrictions may limit a company's institutional appeal, or they may motivate the company to take steps to improve it.

Once the target market of investors has been determined given the corporate image the company plans to project, the company must find ways to reach that market. The company may wish to hire an investor relations firm and prepare a corporate capabilities brochure describing the company and its markets, products, and operations. If the company already advertises its products, the company may change the campaign to incorporate corporate image-building to help build investor interest in the company. Many companies, for instance, now use the power of the Internet to promote the company message with creative web sites.

Management must try to identify securities analysts and members of the business media who follow the industry and make a special effort to reach them, either through personal meetings or by putting them on the company mailing list. Building a strong relationship with the press, both trade publications and the national or local businesses and financial press, will help keep publicity flowing during and after an IPO.

RISKS OF THE IPO

Of the numerous risks associated with an IPO, the most obvious, perhaps, is that the offering will not be completed and the costs incurred will have been wasted. One reason this can happen is that changes in the market or disappointing financial results cause the underwriter to back out. Another risk is that the stock may have to be offered at a lower price per share to attract investors, this may result in either lower proceeds from the offering or greater dilution to current shareholders.

If the public offering is made prematurely, there is the risk of serious long-term consequences. If the company falters shortly after going public, whether because of unstable management, technological difficulties, market forces, the economy, or other reasons, its credibility will be undermined. The company and its executives may even be sued by disgruntled shareholders. It will be difficult to regain investor confidence.

TIMING OF THE IPO

Once the company has weighed all the pros and cons and has decided the best thing for the company is to go public, it must decide if now is the best time to do it. If the capital the company needs is available from nonpublic sources at reasonable cost, it may want to delay going public. If funds raised from other sources can be used to increase the company's growth potential first, the stock eventually issued in an IPO may be more valuable, which might make it possible to raise more capital or sell fewer shares.

Timing is crucial element. The market for initial offerings has been known to fluctuate dramatically, often within a single year. In deciding whether the time is right to go public, a company should ask: Is the mood of the market right? Is the market strong, or is it slumping? Are prices rising or falling? Is trading volume up or down?

Investor acceptance of new issues is cyclical and often not predictable. Infatuation with a particular industry can significantly increase the share price for IPOs in that industry, but the window for new issues for the industry in which the company operates can close unexpectedly just as quickly as it opened.

The complexity of the ever-changing capital market virtually necessitates the advice of an underwriter or investment banker in determining the optimal time to go public. When the market is favorable, many companies go to the market to obtain funds that they do not yet need, simply to eliminate the need to speculate on future market conditions.

CHAPTER 12

PREPARATION MAKES THE DIFFERENCE

One message of this book should already be loud and clear. Take all the time necessary to enter the IPO arena thoroughly prepared. The most successful IPOs are those where the issuing companies had systematically positioned themselves to act like successful public companies months or years in advance. The well-prepared company that has addressed all the issues will be able to move swiftly when the market is right.

ENHANCING THE VALUE OF AN IPO AHEAD OF TIME

Once the company decides to go public, it must be done from a position of maximum strength. Companies whose IPOs were most successful were those that already had attained a superior competitive position at the time of the IPO (Spiess and Pettway, 1997). Among the elements to be considered in preparing the company for a successful IPO is whether potential value can be added by one or more strategic transactions.

A company's transaction strategy must be comprised of much more than an IPO alone. Not only will a well-planned and well-executed transaction add value to the IPO, it also will increase the company's credibility with market analysts and investors. Virtually any successful transaction demonstrates to interested observers that the company can plan and execute a complex strategy. It is well known that the quality of management is a major factor in the decisions of institutional investors about their investments (Miller and Reilly, 1997). Again, the company must look to the Balanced Scorecard to ensure a proper and successful transaction strategy.

Many transactions today can also raise the company's level of comfort with the IPO. When a company has already interacted with institutional investors in, say, a private placement or an acquisition, it has a more sophisticated understanding of their concerns.

There may be a time when either the company or the IPO market is not quite ready for a public offering, but the company still needs capital to sustain growth in the meantime. The answer may be as simple as bridge capital. Bridge capital is financing provided to a company that is expecting to go public within six months to two years. It is often structured to be repaid from the proceeds of the anticipated public offering. Almost any financing alternative can be used as bridge financing, especially venture capital, a private placement, and mezzanine financing. These and other options are discussed in what follows.

Whether the company uses creative transactions to secure bridge financing or to strengthen its competitiveness, there are many ways that can help it enter the IPO market in a stronger position. Among them are acquisitions, venture capital, private placements, mezzanine financing, joint ventures, and recapitalizations.

ACQUISITIONS

A company might choose to undertake an acquisition to buy additional product lines, technologies, geographical focus, distribution channels, or manufacturing capacity. A good acquisition can be quicker and more cost effective than building internally and it can also bring in people with expertise that the company needs. In addition to the obvious advantages of efficiencies of scale, there is also an opportunity to reduce risk by diversifying.

A successful acquisition can add value to an IPO by increasing the momentum of the company's earnings and revenue as well as by adding critical mass. It can demonstrate management's aggressiveness and skill, giving the market evidence of management credibility.

There are four stages to an acquisition:

1. Planning, in which the strategy is created and targets are identified.

2. Valuation.

3. Negotiation.

4. Post-acquisition integration.

    Although every stage is important, the last is most critical and should be carefully anticipated during the planning stage.

The most elusive element in an acquisition is how to make sure that the synergies that were planned come to fruition. Many a company has entered into an acquisition with the best intentions, only to be gravely disappointed in the months and years that follow (AOL Time Warner is the most obvious current example). The difference between success and failure hinges on a variety of factors, but the critical ones are good professional advice and sound management of the integration of the two companies.

VENTURE CAPITAL

Because they are looking to future potential, venture capital firms often invest in companies that do not qualify for other forms of financing. As a result, venture capital is most appropriate for a fast-growth business that has the potential to generate the exceptional returns venture capitalists expect. However, because the basic nature of a venture capital relationship is contingent on the future, the venture capitalist supplying the funds will want some insurance that it will be able to harvest, cash in on, its investment.

An investment of venture capital can take the form of common stock, preferred stock convertible into common stock, or debentures convertible into common stock. Whatever the form, the financial package is structured to allow the venture capitalists to liquidate their investment and realize their profits when the investment matures, which they usually expect within five to seven years. Some agreements call for a public offering after a specified number of years or at the venture capitalist's option. Others provide for a management buy-out option. Still others result in the company being merged into or purchased by another company.

How active or passive a role the venture capitalist plays will vary. Because their investment is predicated on confidence in existing management and on the company's potential, such firms typically do not take over the company's management. Yet because they are the lead investor, they closely monitor company performance and often insist on being represented on the board. This is often a blessing because venture capitalists generally have the business experience to make a meaningful contribution to the company. Should management fail to perform up as promised and expected, however, venture capitalists generally will not hesitate to move in to protect their investment.

Approaching venture capitalists may require more preparation than is required when a company seeks other sources of financing. Recognizing their interest in a particular product or service and their prospective equity stake in its success, the company will put together more detailed plans and projections. The financial plan should explicitly specify the amounts and timing of financing requirements, how all such funds will be applied, year-by-year (and month-by-month for the first one or two years) sales and profit projections, the projected time frame for maturity of the venture, and how the venture capitalist will liquidate the investment and realize a profit. In preparing for the negotiations, the company should also think carefully about how much equity it and the current shareholders are willing to give up, both now and in the future.

Many venture capital firms concentrate on specific industries or stages of investment, such as bridge financing. The valuable contacts, market expertise, and business strategy they can offer as a result of this specialization can be as important as the money they provide, so it is important to seek out potential investors whose skills, experience, goals, and reputations complement the company's.

One of the most critical elements for a successful venture capital relationship is close alignment of the objectives of the company and the venture capitalist. At the very beginning, the two must reach agreement on several key aspects: What are the investment objectives? What are the liquidity needs of the business? How much control is the company willing to give up? Making sure that the company's needs are compatible with the venture capitalist's needs is probably the most critical step to a successful outcome.

PRIVATE PLACEMENTS

Though going public may be feasible eventually, how can a company obtain needed financing now? A private placement, selling stock directly to a few private investors instead of the public at large, can be faster and less expensive than a public stock offering. A private placement is exempt from detailed and time-consuming SEC registration requirements. This is a significant advantage because it reduces paperwork, saves time, and costs far less than an IPO.

Saving time and money for small companies in need of growth capital was exactly what Congress had in mind when it provided for registration exemptions in 1933. The aim was to simplify compliance with securities laws and make it easier for companies to raise capital. The Small Business Investment Incentive Act of 1980 expanded the number of exemptions, and the resulting changes in SEC regulations have made private placements an increasingly popular method of raising capital.

Although exemption is the key word, the company has far from a completely free hand. While the private placement may be exempt from federal regulation, it may not be exempt from registration under state laws. Some require registration, some do not. Also, private placements are not exempt from the antifraud provisions of the securities laws. This means that the company must give potential investors the information they need to make well-informed decisions about the company. Meticulous care must be exercised to neither to omit or misstate facts or to paint them in a rosier hue than they deserve.

Broadly defined, the private placement market includes a wide variety of larger corporate finance transactions, including senior and subordinated debt, asset-backed securities, and equity. Institutional investors, larger corporate issuers, and investment bankers or other corporate finance intermediaries dominate this sophisticated market.

As privately negotiated transactions, private placements can be formulated to meet the specific need of a single company. Amortization schedules for debt securities can be tailored to match anticipated cash flow. By attaching warrants or other equity "kickers," it is possible to

improve returns on debt securities for investors without raising immediate dilution or control implications for current owners. Equity financing has the advantage it requires no current debt servicing, thus con-
serving the company's cash flow for investment in the business.
Creative securities can be structured to minimize the transfer of control
to outside investors.

MEZZANINE FINANCING

If the company is beyond the early growth stage but lacks the resources
from earnings to fund sales growth or capital projects, mezzanine
financing may resolve the dilemma. Although the term can be used to
refer to any private placement of medium-risk capital, mezzanine
financing often describes a subordinated debt instrument used by companies with sales of $5 to $100 million. In addition to a fixed interest
rate, the debt comes with warrants to purchase equity in the company,
typically between 5 and 15 percent. The warrants are what make a
lender more willing to provide financing to a company considered too
high a risk for conventional debt.

Although the fixed interest rate may be relatively low, the interest
combined with the equity provision is designed to give investors a total
return of 25 percent and higher than they would get for collateralized or
other senior debt, but lower than the rate-of-return requirements of a
typical venture capital investor.

Note that, mezzanine investors, like venture capitalists, will want to
cash in the investment at some point. Usually, this can be done through
a buy-back provision. In soliciting mezzanine financing, the company
must ascertain whether it will be able to go public or otherwise be able
to fund the buy-back.

Several capital funds, structured like venture capital funds, specialize in this stage of capital. Other financial institutions also provide mezzanine financing, including insurance companies, finance companies,
and banks.

JOINT VENTURES AND OTHER STRATEGIC ALLIANCES

Regardless of the label, strategic partnership, strategic alliance, or corporate venture, collaboration with a larger, financially stronger company can provide the company with the resources it needs to meet its

goals. A strategic partnership can contribute more than money to the company's success. Depending on the circumstances, the partner also might provide, for example, manufacturing or technological capabilities or marketing agreements, giving the company access to new or expanded distribution channels, particularly in international markets.

Although almost any structure is possible, in a typical strategic partnership, the smaller company sells a minority interest in its business to a larger company. In addition to equity funding, the smaller partner may also expect to benefit from the entrepreneurial talent and ability to innovate. The larger company might gain access to technology, add the partner's product to its product line, or profit from a business opportunity the company may have identified. Because of these benefits, a strategic partner may require a smaller share of equity than an investor seeking only a financial return on investment.

A minority investment by a larger company is only one way to structure a strategic alliance. Other forms of alliances are setting up a separate legal entity as a joint venture, establishing cooperative arrangements for a specific purpose, such as to fund research and development or to exploit an idea or strategy, and a variety of cross-licensing or cross-distribution agreements.

The three most common causes of failed alliances are (1) incompatible partners, (2) unrealistic expectations, and (3) ill-defined objectives (Carter, 1998). In evaluating compatibility, partners should consider management and corporate styles and individual personalities. For example, how can an entrepreneurial partner who is accustomed to quick actions best work with a large firm with a slower, multilayered decision-making process? Where will control be assigned, and how will conflicts be resolved'?

Both parties should assess their objectives and expectations and communicate them in a formal written agreement that defines and quantifies, to the extent possible, timing, measurement criteria for determining the success of the project or relationship, and alternatives for ending the relationship.

Disappointment sometimes occurs when one partner learns that the other might not be the source of the funding that was initially expected. Here again, quantifiable milestones will support more realistic expectations. The ultimate success of a partnership requires that both partners have compatible economic and strategic goals.

RECAPITALIZATIONS

Today's private market offers great opportunities for company recapitalizations. A leveraged recapitalization involves the sale of a substantial part of the company to an outside investor, followed by a borrowing and repurchase of shares from the current owners. The owner receives cash and retains a substantial equity stake, usually from 20 percent to 51 percent, but at least 5 percent. This restructuring of the balance sheet and equity ownership effectively transfers ownership from the current owners to a third party (the "equity sponsor"), using funds borrowed from a bank or a private lender. When properly structured under the accounting rules, a leveraged recapitalization avoids recognition of goodwill and its resulting drag on future earnings.

A recapitalization brings many advantages to the company. It allows management to focus on the operation of the business, and it enhances the company's credibility in the marketplace. It is particularly useful in positioning the company for an IPO by giving access to operational and financial sophistication.

For example, a company might need $30 million from the public market to provide investors with liquidity. Yet taking $30 million in cash from a public offering would not look good to the market. By entering into a leveraged recapitalization in advance of the IPO, the company could borrow the $30 million, using it to pay the debt. This is a typical transaction, one that the market understands and accepts.

FINANCING ALTERNATIVES

Going public is not always the right answer. A wide variety of alternative sources of financing may be available for a company. Which source is best will depend on many different factors, among them the amount required, when it is required, how long the company expects to need it, when the company can repay it, whether the company can afford to service debt, the lifecycle stage the company's is in, and the company's goals and objectives.

CHAPTER 13

UNDERWRITING THE IPO

Selecting the right managing underwriters is a key ingredient for a successful IPO. For some small companies, the reputation of the underwriters can be one of the most important factors investors consider in evaluating the IPO. A variety of firms actively underwrite IPOs. Many of the large brokerage houses have major national investment banking divisions. Smaller firms often specialize in specific industries.

MAKING THE CHOICE

Selecting the managing underwriters best suited to the company's situation, as we discussed in Chapter 3, should begin with the company's self-evaluation, If the company's geographic coverage is national or international, it may be best to retain a national firm to enhance the corporate image in the United States and in select areas abroad. If the company's market is regional, a regional firm may be able to serve equally well.

If the industry is complex, the company may want to seek underwriters who specialize in that particular industry. If the company plans to diversify, through acquisition or internally, it should call upon an investment-banking firm with experience in the new industry. A company can avoid having to repeat the selection process by choosing underwriters that can fill both current and anticipated needs, in the hope of building a long-term professional relationship.

The underwriter must choose to accept responsibility for selling the IPO. Some firms do not handle IPOs or are interested in offerings only above certain minimum amounts. Others may decline based on its assessment of the future prospects of the company or the industry. An underwriter's reputation hangs largely on the success of the offerings it has underwritten. Because underwriters are compensated only if the offering is completed, they will not want to commit time and resources unless they are reasonably confident that the offering will be completed successfully.

Before approaching underwriters, the company should have in hand its formal business plan describing the company, its leaders, its products, its past performance, and its future plans. The business plan will serve both as a brief introduction to the company and as a sales tool for approaching the underwriter. The quality of the business plan will influence the underwriters' initial assessment of the company and its prospects, so the company may wish to get help from its auditors or other advisers in preparing it.

Once the business plan is ready, the next step is to make develop a list of underwriters who appear to meet the criteria the company has set thus far (e.g., national or regional, industry specialization). The company's auditors, bankers, and attorneys can help the company identify those firms and perform a preliminary evaluation of them based upon the following criteria:

- Experience.

- Reputation.

- Syndication and distribution capability.

- Aftermarket support.

RESEARCH CAPABILITY

An extremely important component of building maintaining market interest in an IPO is how well the underwriters analyze and distribute information about the company and the industry. The underwriter's research department should have the resources necessary to produce that information. It should also have a reputation that commands the respect of investors, particularly institutional investors, and the financial community in general.

CONTINUING FINANCIAL ADVISORY SERVICES

The managing underwriter should have the resources to provide the company with continuing investment banking services. This would include assistance in obtaining additional capital as the need arises (whether from private or public sources), advising on proposed mergers or acquisitions, and generally providing a full range of investment banking services.

COST

While the cost of underwriting is substantial and cannot be ignored, it should be a less important criterion in selecting the underwriters than the ones listed above. While it is still in the early stages of evaluating prospective underwriters, a company will not be able to compare costs because commissions and other forms of underwriter's compensation are a matter of negotiation.

Once the company has formally or informally evaluated a number of underwriters, it can make a short list of several underwriters to approach directly. There are varying opinions on how many underwriters a company should negotiate with at the same time. One school of thought warns against "shopping" for underwriters and recommends approaching only one firm at a time. Another viewpoint holds that some "shopping" would be to the company's advantage.

The number of underwriters the company approaches will depend partly on how attractive the company's IPO is. If the offering is small and highly speculative, it may be difficult to find even one investment banker willing to underwrite it. In a relatively small offering, the underwriter's commission also will be modest. Under these circumstances, an underwriter will be less willing to spend a significant amount of time investigating and negotiating with the company unless they are sure of getting the business.

On the other hand, if the IPO is large and likely to be attractive to underwriters, the company may be well advised to approach three or four on a preliminary basis. However, the company must be sure to let them know that it is approaching other underwriters, just as it must be candid about every other aspect of the company and the offering. If the offering is attractive, underwriters will happily spend the necessary time with the company.

Approaching underwriters on the company's short list may be handled either directly by management or indirectly through the company's attorneys, auditors, bankers, or business acquaintances. The company also should consider whether it wishes to retain more than one managing underwriter. Co-managing underwriters, particularly for larger offerings, can be advantageous with respect to initial market coverage, research capabilities, and aftermarket support.

While holding discussions with underwriters, and in selecting managing underwriters, keep in mind that the company will have a fairly intense relationship with the people assigned to the company's account, so company managers should be comfortable with them on a personal level.

WORKING WITH THE UNDERWRITERS

The company will work closely with its managing underwriters in the preliminary stages before the IPO, through the completion of the offering, and long into the future on subsequent public offerings, mergers, or acquisitions.

Underwriters examine a company and its prospects much as an investor would, but far more intensively. Their examination begins with the company's business plan. This document will either spark their interest or lead to rejection, so it should be prepared well to present the company in the best light possible while staying firmly anchored in fact. Here, and in all future dealings with the underwriter, the company must scrupulously avoid any misrepresentation. If underwriters find they have been misled, they will abort the offering, leaving the company with the cost of delay, lost time, and a tarnished reputation.

If the underwriters decide to investigate further, they will delve deeply into the business. They will interview key executives, scrutinize the financial statements, challenge the accounting policies, and examine the financial projections. Often they also will meet with the company's auditors. They will evaluate the company's products in relation to the industry and talk to suppliers and customers in an effort to assess growth potential. The intended use of the proceeds of the offering also will be taken into consideration. In short, they will perform a thorough evaluation of the company to decide whether or not to handle the offering and how to price and promote the offering.

While cost may not be the most important consideration in selecting the managing underwriter, underwriters come at a high price. Their primary source of compensation is a commission on the stock they sell, but they will sometimes request other forms of compensation, such as stock options or warrants. The compensation arrangements should be clear before company and underwriter start with the registration. Some common factors to be considered in negotiating terms with an underwriter are discussed next.

LETTER OF INTENT

The final underwriting agreement is usually not signed until the morning of the day the registration statement is to become effective. Until that time, there is no legal obligation for either the company or the underwriters to proceed with the offering. It would be extremely rare for either an underwriter or a company to abort a public offering after the registration process has begun except under the most unusual circumstances, and then it is typically by mutual consent.

Many underwriters prepare a letter of intent that is signed by the managing underwriter and the company's management. The letter of intent details the underwriter's commission that has been agreed on, the estimated offering price, and other negotiated terms, but it does not create a legal obligation for either the company or the underwriters to proceed with the offering. However, the letter may create a binding obligation for the company to pay certain expenses if the offering is not completed.

TYPES OF UNDERWRITING

The two common types of underwriting agreements are "firm commitment" and "best efforts." In a firm commitment agreement, the underwriters agree to buy all the shares in the offering and then resell them to the public. Any shares not sold to the public are held by the underwriters for their own account. This type of agreement gives the company the most assurance of raising the required funds and is used by most of the larger underwriters.

Often the underwriters are also given an "over-allotment option" that lets them buy a specific number of additional shares from the company if they sell more shares than the underwriting agreement stipulates. Over-allotment options take various forms. In some situations, the company will issue additional shares if the option is exercised. In others, the additional shares are provided from the holdings of other shareholders. The existence of an over-allotment option must be disclosed in the IPO prospectus.

In a best efforts agreement, the underwriters simply agree to use their best efforts to sell the shares on behalf of the company. Some best efforts are all-or-nothing arrangements in which the offering is withdrawn if the shares cannot all be sold. Others set a lower minimum number of shares that must be sold for the offering to be completed.

The obvious drawback of a best efforts underwriting is that the company is not assured of obtaining all the capital it needs, while it still has to assume the responsibilities of being a public company.

OFFERING PRICE

Underwriters generally will not and cannot guarantee an offering price and the total proceeds in advance. The offering price is not finalized until just before the registration statement becomes effective because it must be responsive to current market conditions. Although most underwriters are unwilling to predict an offering price, they will generally estimate a range for the offering price based on market conditions at the time of their estimate. While such estimates are not binding and will change in response to changes in market conditions up to the effective date of the offering, they do reduce the chance of misunderstandings and last-minute surprises.

UNDERWRITING COMMISSION

The underwriting commission, or discount, is generally the single largest expense in a public offering. For recent IPOs, the commission rate has generally been in the range of 6 to 10 percent. Debt offerings generally result in lower commission rates than common stock offerings.

In determining what commission to charge, underwriters consider a number of factors that affect how much effort they will have to expend in selling the shares, among them the size of the offering, market rates for offerings of similar size, the type of underwriting, and the marketability of the shares. There may also be a trade-off between the rate of commission and other forms of compensation, particularly for smaller offerings.

WARRANTS

Some underwriters negotiate for stock warrants in addition to their commission. Warrants are more common with smaller underwriters and smaller offerings. If granting stock warrants can be traded off for a lower commission rate, the obvious advantage is increased net proceeds from the offering, although there will be some dilution of shareholder equity. The company must ensure that an agreement is reached on the number and terms of the warrants in advance to avoid any last-minute misunderstandings.

EXPENSES

It is common, particularly for smaller offerings, for the managing underwriters to request reimbursement for some of their expenses incurred for the IPO. For example, the issuer often reimburses legal fees incurred in the underwriter's review of compliance with state securities laws. These legal fees will increase with the number of states in which the company offers its shares because each state has different filing requirements. Therefore, the company may wish to discuss geographic syndication in the negotiations stage, before the managing underwriters establish the underwriting syndicate. The company may also be able to negotiate a limit to the amount of expenses the company will be required to reimburse.

RIGHTS OF FIRST REFUSAL

Some underwriters will request a right of first refusal on any future stock offerings by the company. While such a request may seem harmless, it can adversely affect future offerings. Other underwriters will be reluctant to invest the time and resources necessary to evaluated a proposed offering if they know they may be preempted by another underwriter's right of first refusal.

If a right of first refusal cannot be avoided, either the company should consider negotiating a time limit after which the right expires or a provision that the right expires any time it is available but not exercised.

PRICING THE STOCK

Determining an appropriate offering price for the securities is one of the most difficult decisions the company and its underwriters will have to make in an IPO. Before tackling that decision, however, the company must decide what type of security to offer.

Most IPOs consist of common stock, but some consist of both common stock and warrants to purchase additional shares of common stock. The other, less usual, possibilities are debt, preferred stock, or units that include common stock and convertible debentures. Generally, it is not practicable to issue only convertible securities unless there is already a public market for the common stock that would be obtained on conversion. Spiess and Pettway (1997) have pointed out some factors to consider in determining how to structure the offering:

- The cash flow consequences of interest for debt and dividend requirements for preferred stock.
- The debt-to-equity ratio that will result in either case.
- The potential dilution stock warrants would introduce.
- The income tax implications of each option.

Though the final pricing decision is not made until just before the underwriting agreement is signed, generally the day before or the morning of the effective date of the registration statement, the background research, comparisons, analysis, and discussions will have begun well in advance of that date.

Offering prices of shares of common stock are often compared based on the price-earnings ratio, one of the most important considerations in comparing a proposed price to other current public offerings or existing public companies in the industry in which the company operates. A variety of other factors must also be considered. The projected impact on earnings that will result from the proposed use of the new funds, the past and projected rate of growth, and the quality of past earnings (e.g., whether they include extraordinary or nonrecurring losses or gains) will all affect the price of the IPO shares.

Dilution—the possibility of decrease in the value of ownership if other shareholders are given an opportunity to exercise warrants, is often an issue. A company's vulnerability to competition, relative management strength, size of the offering, planned acquisitions, and whether or not it is part of a glamour industry also come into play.

In short, pricing the stock is more of an art than a science. The underwriters' experience gives them a good foundation to advise the company on what price would be appropriate. Although it is tempting to set as high a price as possible—particularly if there is to be a secondary offering of the stock owned by current shareholders, overpricing is not a good idea. Underwriters typically advise a company to set a price that will produce an active aftermarket in the shares. Overpricing tends to destroy investor confidence, possibly creating a downward spiral in the price. By pricing to allow for a modest price rise in the immediate aftermarket, a company can stimulate public interest.

Some new issues realize substantial price increases in the early weeks of the aftermarket, leading some to conclude that the offering price was seriously understated. In most cases, however, the price increase is more reflective of undue public optimism than underwriting error. Within a relatively short time the stock price generally returns to the more realistic levels anticipated by the underwriter.

Finally, a company must decide on how many shares will be offered. To support active trading in the aftermarket, most underwriters believe a minimum of 800,000 to a million shares are necessary to allow for sufficiently broad distribution. Because the number of shares offered and the offering price are directly related, many companies are advised to split their stock to establish an appropriate number of shares for the offering. Stock splits also are often motivated by a need to bring the offering price within an acceptable range, which many consider to be between $5 and $20 per share, depending on the industry. Stock splits do not affect the price-earnings multiple.

CHAPTER 14

AFTER THE OFFERING

Going public will subject a company and its shareholders, directors, and executives to a variety of new responsibilities. Some of these relate to the requirements of the securities laws, others to the way the company must now conduct its affairs. Because some of the laws to which the company is now subject are extremely technical and complex, it will need the advice of attorneys and auditors to comply effectively with all the relevant provisions.

PERIODIC REPORTING GENERALLY

One of the first reports that must be filed after a registered public offering is a Form SR periodic report on how the proceeds of the offering have been used. Form SRs must be filed within 10 days after the end of the first three-month period following the effective date of the registration statement and then within 10 days after the end of each subsequent six-month period. The final report is due 10 days After the offering ends or proceeds of the offering are fully applied, whichever is later.

Form SR is a short question-and-answer form on which the company must report sales of securities, use of the net proceeds, and whether the use of the proceeds is materially different from that described in the prospectus, if it is, the company must provide reasons for the change.

As a newly public company that has filed a 1933 Securities Act registration statement, the company is immediately subject to the periodic reporting requirements of the Securities Act of 1934, Section 15(d). If the company's shares are trading on a national securities exchange or on Nasdaq, or if there are more than 500 shareholders of any class of the company's shares and the company reported more than $5 million in assets, the company must also register under the 1934 Act by filing a Form 8-A. This form incorporates most information by reference from the registration statement and periodic report to the SEC. The 1934 Act registration usually becomes effective once the exchange on which the shares are traded has approved the listing application and notified the SEC.

Although the company must always file periodic reports for the first fiscal year, the duty to file such reports may be thereafter suspended after that if there are fewer than 300 shareholders of the class of securities registered, or if after the first two fiscal years following the offering, there are fewer than 500 shareholders and the company reported less than $5 million in assets on the last day of each of the previous three years. Suspension under these options is immediate once the company files Form 15 with the SEC. Regardless of the number of shareholders, however, a company whose shares are listed on a national securities exchange or on Nasdaq must remain subject to the periodic reporting requirements.

The importance of complying with the periodic reporting requirements cannot be overemphasized. Periodic reports are the primary way a company communicates with its shareholders and other members of the financial community. Poorly prepared, incomplete, or late reports may adversely affect its investor and public relations. It may also draw SEC sanctions, generate ill will among SEC staff toward the company, and could even preclude future use of certain simplified registration forms.

FORM 10-K

The 10-K is the primary report for annually updating much of the information in the original registration statement. The disclosure requirements are similar to those of the S-1 registration statement. Like the registration statement, the form is merely a guide, not a blank form to be filled in. The 10-K is due within 90 days after the end of the fiscal year.

Much of the information required in the 10-K is also required in other SEC filings or in the annual report to shareholders prescribed by the SEC's proxy requirements. Instead of repeating information that has already been submitted in previous SEC filings or the annual report, each 10-K references the previous filing or annual report. For example, a company may attached to the 10-K as an exhibit a copy of the annual report containing the audited financial statements rather than repeating the same information in the 10-K.

FORM 10-Q

The 10-Q quarterly report is a summary containing quarterly unaudited financial statements and management's discussion of the company's financial condition and operations. Certain specified events (e.g., legal proceedings, changes in the terms of securities, certain defaults, and matters submitted to a shareholder's vote) must also be disclosed in the 10-Q. Form 10-Q must be filed within 45 days after the end of each of the first three fiscal quarters.

FORM 8-K

After specified significant events—change in control, acquisition or disposition of significant assets, bankruptcy or receivership, change in independent auditors, resignation of a director, or any other event considered of importance to shareholders—companies must file the Form 8-K. The form must usually be filed within 15 days of the reportable event, but a change in independent auditors or the resignation of a director must be reported within five business days. The form specifies minimum disclosures that must be made about each event.

PERIODIC REPORTING UNDER THE 1934 ACT

As I've already mentioned, once a company completes an IPO and registers with an exchange, it becomes subject to the periodic reporting requirements of the 1934 Securities Exchange Act. What is required for the registrant's first 1934 Act filing, and when, depends on whether the first report to be filed is a Form 10-Q or Form 10-K and on which provision of the 1934 Act governs the registrant's periodic reporting.

If the first report is a quarterly one, the Form 10-Q must be filed within 45 days of the effective date of the IPO registration statement or before the date on which it would have been required for the latest fiscal quarter if the firm was already required to file it, whichever is later. For example, after an IPO for a calendar year registrant that is declared effective on July 15, the first Form 10-Q, covering the three- and six-month periods ended June 30, would be due August 29, the 45th day after the date of the registration statement.

In situations where the first report to be filed by a new registrant is a Form 10-K, the timing and type of report will be determined by whether the registrant's reporting is governed by Section 12 or by Section 15 of the 1934 Act. Companies governed by Section 12 are those that are either listed on a national exchange or have more than 500 shareholders and $5 million in assets. Those governed by Section 15 are those that do not meet the size test and are subject to the 1934 Act only by virtue of a 1933 Act registered public offering.

Registrants governed by Section 12 of the 1934 Act must file their complete Form 10-K with the SEC within 90 days of the end of their fiscal year (Rule 13a-1 under the 1934 Act). Registrants filing under Section 15 whose IPO registration statement did not contain financial statements for the firms last full fiscal year (or the life of the registrant, that is less than a full fiscal year) preceding the fiscal year in which the registration statement became effective must, within 90 days after the effective date, file with the SEC a special report that contains financial statements for the relevant period that meet the requirements for annual reports of the registrant (Rule 15d-2 under the 1934 Act). This report need contain only financial statements for the year in question. There is no requirement for disclosures pursuant to Regulation S-K.

PUBLIC AND INVESTOR RELATIONS

Being a new public company is a decidedly mixed blessing. On the one hand, there has been a capital infusion into the company. On the other, the company has acquired a group of shareholders, often numbering in the hundreds or thousands, each of whom has a valid and vital interest in the company's success. Either directly or relying on securities analysts and the financial press, these shareholders will critically, and constantly, evaluate the performance of management. They will be measuring the company's progress not only in comparison to competitors and to industry standards, but also against their own unique expectations (Bray and Gompers, 1997).

The company's new responsibility to shareholders has far-reaching implications for how it conducts its business. Facing the company's owner is now much more complicated than simply looking in the mirror, or even walking into the corner office. The new, stronger obligation to keep the owners informed must be fulfilled through annual and quarterly reports, proxy statements, press releases, direct mailings, and shareholders' meetings.

A public company must promptly disclose any significant events or developments that concern the company, positive or negative. It must take particular care that material information is disclosed publicly and not leaked, either intentionally or inadvertently.

There is also a new measure of the company's performance—the share price—and, from the shareholders' perspective, this is the critical measure. New public companies often enjoy high share prices at first, partly because of investor interest in IPOs and the press attention that often attends a company's going public. Unless that initial market interest in the company is sustained after the public offering, however, the euphoria will soon disappear and with it part of the value of the company's shares. Keeping a positive image of the company before the financial community and investors requires a conscious effort by management.

INVESTOR RELATIONS

To keep the market interested in its securities, a company must direct its promotional efforts not only at those already invested in the company—the shareholders—but also at potential investors. There are a variety of effective ways to reach this financial community.

Securities analysts play a vital role. They are often part of the research departments of brokerage houses and investment banking arms, and so their assessments of the company will influence the investment advice these organizations provide to their clients.

Securities analysts not only analyze annual reports and other published information, they will also interview management to delve more deeply into a company's operations, plans, and prospects. Management should welcome such interviews, and even initiate them if that can be done.

Many cities have local societies of securities analysts who meet regularly to hear presentations from the managers of public companies. These forums give management an opportunity to promote the company, disseminate information on its plans, and respond to analysts'questions. Opportunities to appear before these groups should be welcomed.

Many companies prepare a corporate brochure and update it regularly both for security analyst presentations and for general corporate publicity. These brochures usually describe the company and its products or services, give information on its management team, and provide selected financial data, as well as any other information that might help investors and analyst view the company favorably.

PUBLIC RELATIONS

Maintaining a strong, positive image within the community, whether local, regional, or national, will serve the company well. In addition to reinforcing its reputation among shareholders and potential investors, it will help attract and retain employees, influence customer and consumer purchase decisions, and create goodwill that can benefit the company indirectly in a variety of ways.

Many companies retain public relations consultants to assist them. A good public relations program can be integrated with product advertising but should also be directed at building a corporate image beyond the company's specific products or services.

SHORT-TERM PROFITS AND LONG-TERM GROWTH

One of the ever-present issues facing public companies is the pressure to grow short-term earnings. There is often a temptation to maintain current share prices by sacrificing long-term profitability. Unfortunately, the financial markets generally react adversely to reports of reduced earnings, whether or not the underlying long-term strategic decisions are sound.

This unfortunate dilemma doesn't necessarily mean that investors are shortsighted. Rather, it reflects the realities of the financial markets. It also underlines the importance of a strong investor relations program. As noted economist John Maynard Keynes once said, "We have reached the third degree where one devotes one's intelligence to anticipating what average opinion expects the average opinion to be."

There is no easy solution to the dilemma. The challenge is to craft a sound business strategy that achieves a balance between short and long term needs, and then communicate that strategy clearly to shareholders, the financial community, and to the extent possible the public.

THE LAW BEYOND THE REPORTING REQUIREMENTS

Beyond the reporting required under the securities laws, a public company is also subject to a variety of other laws and their related regulations that did not apply when the company was privately held.

PROXY SOLICITATION

Because the shareholders of most public companies are widely dispersed and rarely attend shareholders'meetings, company management usually solicits from them proxies that give the managers the authority to vote shareholders'stock at the annual shareholders' meeting. Proxies typically account for the majority of votes cast at these meetings.

The proxy rules apply only to companies governed by Section 12 of the 1934 Act, those either listed on a national exchange or having more than 500 shareholders and $5 million in assets. They do not apply to those governed by Section 15, unlisted companies that do not meet the size test.

The SEC requires that before proxies may be solicited, a proxy statement must be provided to shareholders. Its content, which is regulated by the SEC, varies according to what is to be voted on. If directors are being elected, the proxy statement must be accompanied by the annual report, including financial statements. In fact when there are elections an information statement similar to a proxy statement must be furnished to shareholders even if no proxies are solicited, but companies listed on the New York or American stock exchanges are required to solicit proxies. The NASD requires national market system issuers with securities quoted on Nasdaq to solicit proxies for all shareholders meetings.

TENDER OFFERS AND ACTIONS BY SHAREHOLDERS OWN 5 PERCENT OR MORE

The SEC regulates both the mechanics for making tender offers and the procedures for management to resist them. Moreover, shareholders or groups of shareholders acting together who acquire 5 percent or more of a company's shares or who make a tender offer that could bring them 5 percent or more ownership have to meet specified disclosure requirements. Reports must not only be filed with the SEC but must also be given to both the company and any stock exchanges on which the shares are listed.

The information that must be given in these reports is generally the identity and background of the purchasers, the source and amount of funds used in the purchase, the purpose of the transaction, and the number of shares ultimately owned. As with the proxy solicitation rules, the tender offer rules do not apply to Section 15 companies, which are subject to the 1934 Act only by virtue of a 1933 registered public offering.

INSIDER TRADING AND SHORT-SWING PROFITS

All directors and officers of a company and all shareholders owning 10 percent or more of the shares, are required to report their holdings to the SEC on specified forms within certain time limits. Any changes in those holdings must also be reported.

To prevent the unfair use of inside information, these parties are also subject to the short-swing profits provisions of the 1934 Act. The Act applies to any profits realized by insiders on the purchase and sale, or sale and purchase, of any of the company's securities within a six-month period, whether or not those transactions were based on insider information. Insiders who do this are required to turn over to the company an amount equal to the difference between the highest sale price and the lowest purchase price within the six-month period, without any offset for losses. If the company does not sue the insider to recover those profits, any shareholder may do so on behalf of the company.

The 1934 Act further prohibits insiders from short selling, selling shares that they do not own, and from selling shares that they own but do not deliver within twenty days after the sale (this is referred to as "short sales against the box"). It is also unlawful for anyone to trade in any securities on the basis of insider information. This applies equally to those directly privy to inside information (e.g., directors, officers, employees) and to anyone they tip off before the information is made public. Bother the insider (whether or not he or she benefits personally) and the "tippee" may be liable for damages to everyone who traded in the security during the period of such illegal insider trading.

The newly public company, then, should put in place controls to protect the confidentiality of sensitive information, making sure that anyone who might become privy to such information is well aware of the proscription not just of trading on but also of conveying such information. For that reason, it is often advisable to coordinate all press statements and communications, whether with analysts, reporters, or other publics, through a single individual.

SALE OF RESTRICTED AND CONTROL STOCK

Controlling shareholders, as I have said, are not free to sell their shares at will in the public markets. They must sell either through a registered secondary offering or in reliance on a specified exemption. Similarly, shares acquired in most private placements are considered "restricted stock" that is subject to resale restrictions designed to ensure that the private placement was not simply one step in a broader public distribution.

To clarify the restrictions on sales of restricted and control stock, the SEC in 1972 adopted Rule 144 to provide a "safe harbor" for such sales. Essentially, it allows controlling shareholders, and holders of restricted stock who have held the stock for two years after it was fully paid for, to sell up to the greater of the following in any three-month period:

• One percent of the securities of that class that are outstanding, or

• The average weekly trading volume, if the security is quoted on Nasdaq or listed on a national exchange.

Restricted stock not held by a controlling shareholder becomes free of most resale restrictions after a three-year holding period, again measured from the date the stock was fully paid for. The SEC has interpreted payment in full to include, for example, certain notes accepted in payment under stock option or stock purchase plans.

Other provisions of Rule 144 relate to combining sales by certain affiliated persons for purposes of the rule, limitations on brokerage commissions, and SEC notification requirements for sales of more than 500 shares or $10,000 in value in a three-month period. Because Rule 144 is so complex, it is a good idea to consult with an attorney before undertaking any sale that might fall under the rule.

EXCHANGE LISTING VERSUS NASDAQ LISTING

In the past, almost all companies going public hoped eventually to be listed on the New York or American stock exchanges. That is no longer the case. Today, an increasing number of companies that would qualify for listing on a floor-based market choose to have their securities listed on the Nasdaq National Market, a screen-based market. New public companies must now consider the relative benefits of listing on an exchange versus Nasdaq:

- Marketability and collateral value are generally considered enhanced by a stock exchange listing because market values can be readily determined and transactions can be consummated more quickly. However, the Nasdaq National Market offers the same real-time trade reporting and automated transaction confirmation, and it enables buyers and sellers to be matched just as quickly.

- A certain prestige is attached to companies listed on a national securities exchange, but how much that influences decisions by investors, creditors, analysts, and others is open to question. On the other hand, the Nasdaq has come to be associated with growth companies and those that are technologically advanced.

- Security prices published in major newspapers used to be limited generally to listed companies, but major newspapers now also print similar information for many Nasdaq National Market securities.

- Some institutional investors are limited to investing in national exchange securities, and others may find listed securities more attractive. To the extent that stock exchange listing increases the marketability of large blocks of shares, institutional investors may be more inclined to invest in these securities.

Companies must meet qualification requirements for listing on either a national exchange or the Nasdaq National Market. The New York Exchange requires, for example, that a company have pretax earnings of $2.5 million in the latest fiscal year and a market value of listed securities of at least of $18 million. It also has minimum requirements for number of shares outstanding, trading volume, and number of shareholders. NYSE companies are also subject to their listing agreement, which deals with such matters as timely disclosure and proxy solicitations. The obligations imposed by the Amex and the regional exchanges are generally less onerous than they are for the New York Stock Exchange or the Nasdaq National Market.

A company considering having its securities listed on Nasdaq should consider seeking a Nasdaq National Market listing. This listing increases the visibility of the company's securities and may make them more attractive to institutional investors. To qualify, a company must satisfy shareholder reporting, independent director, and audit criteria, including minimums on the number of publicly held shares and market value.

CHAPTER 15

WHAT DOES THE FUTURE HOLD?

Now we will turn our attention to the long-term effects on the United States economy and stock prices of IPOs. As the NASDAQ is a technology-heavy market, such effects are especially relevant to that exchange.

Two factors of great relevance are (1) global integration of economic markets and (2) the pricing of Internet-based stocks. This chapter will examine theses issues. Following these examinations, the effects on the United States economy and financial markets in light of the economic events in 2000 and 2001 will be investigated and assessed.

INTRODUCTION

In the latter half of 2000, the unprecedented bull market in the United States began to falter. By the end of the year, market price volatility gave way to a steady downward trend in stock market prices. During the first calendar quarter in 2001, the downward trend in stock prices continued, and observers began to speak of the development of a bear market.

In the latter half of 2000, when stock market price volatility appeared, there were no apparent serious problems in the general economy. By the end of 2000, however, the economy was showing signs of strain.

The economy enjoyed an almost unprecedented boom from 1995 through most of 2000. One of the signal characteristics of the economy during 1999 and 2000 was soaring investor interest in dot-com firms with little history and foundations of sand. These conditions, together with continual predictions of recession by the new Bush administration led the Federal Reserve to initiate what became a series of interest rate reductions. The trend in stock prices leveled in the second calendar quarter of 2001. However, volatility still remained.

The stock market is a barometer of confidence in the future of the economy. When confidence is high, the stock market tends to rise, increasing the wealth of those with funds invested. As wealth rises, so too does consumption, causing the economy to expand. Historically, stock market price declines have preceded recessions. Thus, stock market indexes serve as leading indicators of future economic activity. However, from 1995 to mid-2000 there had been increasing concerns over the future of the stock market. A few wise observers predicted a long-term bear market, others long-term price stagnation, and still others a renewed bull market. Much of the concern centered on the technology-based NASDAQ.

Taking a closer look at this situation, two factors of great relevance emerged (1) global integration of economic markets and (2) the pricing of Internet-based stocks. The following discussions will examine these issues in more detail.

GLOBAL INTEGRATION

Global financial markets are integrating into a single financial marketplace rapidly. Increasingly, the process is drawing in developing countries. Advances in communications and information technology, deregulation of financial markets, and the rising importance of institutional investors that are able and willing to invest internationally are driving the process of global integration.

The globalization of financial markets, together with new forms of investment, increases the number of channels that transmit systemic shocks across borders and sectors and the speed at which these shocks travel. At the same time, it reduces the transparency of the marketplace. Hisashi Owada, Japanese Permanent Representative to the United Nations, observed that:

"The recent financial crises in Asia has demonstrated the need for securing a harmonious and orderly process for the integration of developing countries into the world economy in this age of globalization. Without a successful integration of developing countries, the world economy itself can suffer from the malfunctioning of the system. In this respect, it is imperative to address the issue of global financial integration and development both from the short-term and issue-specific perspective for financial crises and from long-term and comprehensive perspective for development."

The International Bank for Reconstruction and Development noted in 1999 that investors are concerned with the unreliability of emerging markets in three main areas (1) market infrastructure, (2) protection of property rights, in particular those of minority shareholders and (3) disclosure of market and company information and control of abusive market practices. International standards for financial markets are required.

The objective is a regulatory model based on disclosure and self-regulation. Nevertheless, the International Bank for Reconstruction and Development considers that government regulation of the financial markets will continue to have a vital role to play. Government oversight is especially critical, as is governmental participation in the development of the required basic legal structures.

Broad international agreement exists on the desirability of financial liberalization and global financial integration. Important differences exist, however, as to the appropriate structure and standards of global financial integration. Most importantly, the requirement is for mechanisms structured to provide safeguards when the system breaks down as occurred in several Asian economies in 1997.

In a globally integrated economy, however, sound domestic policies alone are insufficient to ensure sustained economic growth and avoidance of external shocks, particularly of a financial nature. There is also a need for a favorable international environment and coherence in macro-economic policies, particularly among the worlds leading economies. Inconsistencies in national policies are likely to cause disturbances in financial markets if they continue uncorrected for some time. The establishment of international financial standards is crucial to the stability of a globally integrated financial system.

Globally, controls on many economic sectors and activities are being relaxed as part of a trend towards more liberalized economies and greater reliance on market forces rather than government intervention. The financial sector, however, continues to be viewed as deserving of special consideration due to its central role in the national economy and the far-reaching damage that financial disruption caused (e.g., imprudent lending). Controls on the financial sector at the national level have thus far been seen as essential to reducing those risks to the economy as a whole. In a financially integrated world, such controls are also seen as necessary for increasing international confidence in the domestic financial system and thereby attracting external capital flows.

The Bank for International Settlements (BIS) has formed three committees that are working on standards for a globally integrated financial system. These committees report to the central bank governors of the Group of Ten, the Euro-Currency Standing Committee, and the Committee on Payment and Settlement Systems. The recommendations of these committees are non-binding, as responsibility for introducing and enforcing the agreed regulations rests with the national legislative bodies.

PRICING OF NEW PRIVATE COMPANIES

The valuation process for new private companies occurs in two phases. The first phase is the pricing evaluation. The objective of this phase is to determine the initial offering price for shares in the new company. The second phase is the market evaluation. The results of this phase reflect the actual worth of the new company based on the market's response to the company's initial public offering price.

VALUATION TOOLS AND DECISION-MAKING PROCESSES

Brokers consider several factors in both the setting and valuation of an IPO price. Among these factors are the following:

- The past performance of the issuing corporation.

- Current financial and marketing positions of the issuing corporation as of the date of the IPO.

• The future outlook of the issuing corporation.

• Trends and conditions in the equity market at the time of the IPO issue.

• The experiences of comparable corporation in the same industry as the issuing corporation.

• Demand for stock in the issuing corporation.

A traditional model applied to the pricing of an IPO is the comparable firm approach. This approach involves a four-step process, which includes:

1. Identify publicly traded companies similar to the testing corporation.

2. Compare the relative performance and future outlook for the issuing corporation and the comparable public firms.

3. Analyze the market pricing mechanism for each comparable public firm.

4. Set a price for the issuing corporation IPO based on the findings of two and three above.

With respect to market pricing mechanisms, the valuation analysis must provide answers to three questions. First, which market multiples are used by the comparable firms for pricing? Consistently, profitable companies tend to price off their P/E or price-to-cash-flow ratios, while unprofitable or unpredictable firms tend to price off book value. Second, are any unique expectations or circumstances reflected in how the market prices each comparable firm? Factors such as aggressive growth expectations, depression due to recent poor performance, or a host of special circumstances—takeover rumors, pending litigation, valuable real estate holdings, a new patent application, an approaching retirement—can skew a stock's price and weaken comparability. Third, how do the current stock prices of each comparable firm compare to their historic prices? Do the current specific multiples and general market multiples fall near the high or low end of their historical ranges, and do they continue or reverse a trend?

The *Capital Asset Pricing Model* (CAPM) is frequently used to assess the equity value of a corporation issuing an IPO for purposes of pricing the IPO. I believe that securities prices are the result of different analyses of somewhat different sets of information, along with different conditions and preferences relevant for various investors. One analyst's estimates of risk and return for a security are likely to differ from those of other analysts. Since both risk and return are subjective estimates dealing with the future, there is ample room for disagreement. These differences make it impossible to categorically measure risk and return and the relationship between them. The CAPM was developed as a simple, yet powerful description of the relationship between risk and return in an efficient market.

More definitively, the CAPM is based on the relationship between the risk of a specific security and the overall risk of the market. This relationship is known as the beta. The beta coefficient of a security is used to determine the level of the market risk premium of a specific security, how much additional return must an investor anticipate receiving from a risky security in order to justify holding it in lieu of a less risky asset, which is generally presumed to be a Treasury instrument.

The CAPM is used to determine the level of the market risk premium. The CAPM postulates that the expected risk premium on each investment is proportional to its beta—each investment should lie on the sloping market line connecting Treasury bills and the market portfolio. The basic assumptions of the CAPM are as follows:

- All investors are sing-period, expected utility of terminal wealth maximizers who choose among alternative portfolios on the basis of means and standard deviations of portfolio returns.

- All investors can borrow or lend an unlimited amount at a given risk-free rate of interest, and there are no restrictions on short sales of any asset.

- All investors have identical estimates of the means, variances, and co-variances of return among all assets. This assumption means that all investors have homogeneous expectations.

- All assets are perfectly divisible and perfectly liquid—marketable at the going price—and there are no transaction costs.

- There are no taxes. As is often true of the assumptions incorporated in the securities analysis models, this one is not relevant to the so-called real world.

- All investors are price takers, that is, all investors assume their own buying and selling will not affect stock prices.

- The quantities of all assets are given. This assumption, additionally, is one that is often difficult to fulfill in real world situations.

Although it is, at once, obvious that several of the basic assumptions have little or no relevance to the actual conditions that are encountered by investors, the assumptions do permit the derivation of relationships between specific securities and the market as a whole. Thus, the derived risk premium will likely be valid, although the model would not likely be successful in the derivation of a base price for the security. Which, it must be added, is not the purpose of the CAPM.

If the theoretical assumptions of the CAPM can be accepted, and if values can be assigned to a risk-free rate of return and to the market price of risk, then the risk premium can be expressed as being proportional to the expected rate of return on a market index. While the CAPM is relatively simple and straightforward as a descriptor of the risk/return relationship, it is evident that, in practice, some inapplicable problems will be encountered.

The essential elements in the functioning of the CAPM are the market portfolio, the capital market line, the security market line, and the beta coefficient. The market portfolio is a combination of all securities active in a market. Each of these securities are included in the market portfolio in proportion to the market value of the volume of shares outstanding.

In our "fictitious" world of the CAPM, it is a simple matter to determine the relationship between portfolio risk and return. Applying the capital market line concept makes this determination. Preferred investment strategies plot along a line, representing alternative combinations of risk and return obtainable by combining market portfolio with borrowing or lending at the risk-free rate of interest.

All investment strategies other than those combining market portfolio and the risk-free rate of interest in an optimal manner would be expected to fall below the capital market line. The slope of the capital market line can be viewed as the reward per unit of risk borne, and equals the difference between the expected return of the market portfolio and that of the risk-free security divided by the difference in their risks.

The capital market line develops the capital asset pricing model with respect to portfolios. The security market line develops the model with respect to specific individual securities. Under the assumptions of the capital asset pricing model, all securities and portfolios plot on a security market line going through a point representing the so-called "risk free" rate of interest.

The beta value for the risk-free security is 0.0 and every security with a beta value of zero "should provide" an expected return equal to the risk-free interest rate. If the beta value for the market portfolio is 1.0, every security with such a beta should be priced to give an expected return of the market. Therefore, every security with a beta of 0.5 should be priced to give an expected return of half the market price.

One of the principal disadvantages of using the CAPM is that it is based on expected conditions, while the only actual data available is past data. Difficulties are also encountered in the precise formulation of the risk premiums.

On the positive side for the CAPM, is the fact that it integrates the evaluation of the investments with the capital market's evaluation of investments with claims against such investments. An advantage of the CAPM is the fact that it provides a manageable way of thinking about the required return on a risky investment. That being said, however, one must still consider the limitations of the model via the assumptions behind the CAPM. One should always be concerned with these limitations. The CAPM provides an alternative no other model offers, however, the limitations do not allow for an entirely "balanced" approach to the valuation of a security. In the future I believe we will have much better theories. However, I will be very surprised if such future theories do not still insist on the crucial distinction between diversifiable and non-diversifiable risk, which is the main idea underlying the CAPM.

Another approach to the setting and evaluation of IPO pricing is *Shareholder Value Analysis* (SVA). Traditional approaches to setting and assessing IPO prices rely on applying key multiples of comparable publicly traded peers to the IPO candidate. The difficulty with this approach is finding truly comparable public peer multiples. Multiples should match only if the comparable public company has identical prospects for growth and profitability, identical investment requirements, and identical accounting procedures. It is unlikely that such a timely comparable peer exists.

The SVA theory is based on the fact that the value of any asset, whether it is a mortgage or equity in an IPO, depends on the magnitude, timing, and degree of uncertainty of its future cash flows. SVA calculates the value of a company by discounting its expected future cash flows using a rate that reflects the company's risk.

The object of the pricing of an IPO is to obtain a fair price for the issuance. A fair price will enhance the probability that investors in the IPO will realize gains both initially and over the long-term, while simultaneously assuring the success of the IPO for the issuing corporation. Issuing corporations, therefore, should not necessarily pursue obtaining the maximum price for the IPO. To state that an IPO valuation price was either too high or too low, would be a matter of judgment. Additionally, it leaves the company post offerings of shares without shareholder apprehension over the price being requested. Therefore, a decision criterion must be established to determine whether an IPO price is either too high or too low.

Underwriters typically advise that an IPO be priced approximately 10 percent below the projected post-offering price. This pricing would allow for immediate appreciation of the stock issuance and would encourage buyers to purchase the stock at a small discount. This approach would obviously lead to increased demand for the equity shares offered. The increased demand, in turn, strengthens to post-offering price of the stock.

Not all would agree with the intentional under-pricing approach of the IPO shares. Knowing, as we do at this point, that unusually high returns accrue to investors on IPOs immediately after the offering, would indicate a more aggressive overall approach. While one must acknowledge the argument that some degree of under pricing is necessary to attract enough investors to an unknown entity and because such an approach to IPO pricing should cause investors to be prepared to support the issuer's subsequent capital needs. I personally do not find this argument convincing, for in an efficient market, only a fair return, not an extraordinary one, will be required to earn the goodwill and attention of the financial community. This, in turn begs the question, would there really be dozens of under-subscribed IPOs if investors no longer expected abnormally high returns?

I believe that such under pricing of IPOs is motivated primarily by the desire of firm insiders to induce information production about their firm. Insiders have private information about the quality of their firm's projects. Outsiders may acquire information at a cost to reduce this information asymmetry. The firm (or its insiders) sells stock in an IPO and generally again in a second offering, which is made after trading begins in the secondary market. Insiders of high-value firms are motivated to maximize outsider information production so that this information will be reflected in the secondary market price of their firm's equity, increasing its expected value. However, since information production is costly, only a lower IPO share price will induce more outsiders to produce information. The equilibrium initial offer price, which may involve under-pricing under certain conditions, emerges from this tradeoff.

Research has documented (Lee, 1999) that IPOs that are the most over-subscribed tend to be those characterized by the highest level of under pricing. The degree of under pricing is larger for those issuing corporations whose offers are more costly to evaluate. Issuing corporations are motivated to under price the IPO because by doing so, it has typically been found, a greater combined proceeds from the initial and second offerings can be obtained.

Corporations preparing to issue and IPO receive advice on pricing from many sources, including investment banks, underwriters, attorneys, accountants, and other entities. Many of the entities making pricing recommendations have interests in the IPO, which may cause their pricing recommendations to be biased. Because a pricing recommendation is biased does not mean that it is necessarily incorrect. This type of situation, however, does mean that the issuing corporation should identify and consider the nature of such bias when IPO pricing decisions are made.

The investment bank selected to underwrite and distribute an IPO is critical to the success of an IPO. The investment banker selected to handle a corporation's IPO should have experience with the particular industry in which the issuing corporation functions. If such is not the case, the investment banker may not provide the best pricing and distribution advice for the IPO. Further, the investment analyst assigned by the investment bank to an IPO issue should be highly regarded by institutional investors. Otherwise, the IPO may not be fully subscribed.

Institutional investors have been critical to the success of an IPO. Issuing corporations and investment bankers underwriting and distributing an issue depend heavily on institutional investors to fully subscribe an IPO. More recently, however, small investors are beginning to play a larger role in the success of IPOs after the crash of all the "dotcom" companies. Even now, however, institutional investors remain the key to the success of an IPO.

The IPO of Starbucks Coffee in 1994 provides an illustration of the role of institutional investors in the success of IPOs. Institutional investors were allocated 45 percent, retail investors 35 percent, international investors 15 percent, and Starbucks employees a five percent share. Through this offering, the Starbucks institutional investor was able, from this author's point of view, to establish the primary factors for the success of the IPO.

I consider four primary factors for success of an IPO to be that this issuance (1) provides the capital being sought by the issuing corporation, (2) ensures the liquidity of the issuing corporation, (3) generates a public awareness of the issuing corporation, and (4) enhances stakeholder value. The pricing of an IPO affects directly the level of capital generated, the liquidity of the issuing corporation, and the enhancements of shareholder value. IPO pricing is crucial, because a price that is either too high or too low may cause investors to shy away from the issue.

Electronic businesses (e-businesses), especially the "dot-com" firms, which were so highly valued in the late 1990's, were evaluated from a different investment perspective—through a different lens than is used to evaluate investment in firms functioning in more traditional venues. An e-business may be defined as almost any firm that derives most of its revenues through on-line transactions, while the dot-com subtype of e-business typically has no-offline presence.

Investments in more traditional businesses are normally evaluated through assessments of performance within the contexts performance, risk, and return. Performance assessments emphasize, among other characteristics, sales growth and profitability, while risk assessments emphasize, among other thing, liquidity, financial-leverage, and return assessment emphasizes earnings per share and dividends per share. The investment evaluation of the dot-com companies seemed to emphasize revenue growth, revenue growth, and revenue growth.

With respect to the stock markets, the absurdities of the Internet IPO bubble I believe will not be repeated and the markets will recover stability and growth.

IPO RESEARCH FINDINGS

In undertaking to write this book, I did some preliminary research in addition to reading thoroughly in the literature. I found a wealth of information that managers might take into account in deciding whether to go with an IPO.

METHODOLOGY

Initially, data sources were used to identify IPOs to be analyzed, then criteria was established for the sample selection, and finally, a statistical model was developed.

DATA SOURCES

The data for this research consists primarily of secondary data, mainly stock prices, compiled from three independent sources (1) *Ward's Business Directory*, (2) *Investment Dealers' Digest Information Services,* and (3) the World Wide Web's Online Historical Stock Quotes Database.

I used the historical data to identify IPOs floated between 1996 and 2002. Other researchers, such as Loughran and Ritter (2002) and Barry and Jennings (2000), have also used the *Investment Dealers' Digest Information Services*, which compiles information about companies at the time of their offering, such as IPO underwriter, expected bid price, date of the offering, and amount of the offering.

The Web's Historical Stock Price database offers a variety of financial information, including stock prices on any given date. *Ward's Business Directory* offers industry information ranked by sales within each four digit Standard Industrial Code (SIC). Ward's was used to identify non-IPO companies that went under or performed reverse stock splits and that were similar in size and industry to the IPOs being analyzed.

SAMPLE SELECTION

The criteria for the sample were all firms that:

- Had an IPO from January 1, 1998, though December 31, 2000.

- Had an initial offer price of $5.00.

- Raised at least $2 million in revenue from the IPO.

Similar non-IPOs were selected by the closest industry code and sales ranking to the IPO being analyzed.

Investment Dealers' Digest listed a total of 895 IPOs for the specified time period. Of these, 52 were eliminated either because the initial offer price was less than $5.00 or the IPO raised less than $2 million (sometimes both), and 126 others were dropped from the study because the IPO was a unit offering with warrants. Another 255 firms were dropped because it was not possible to find non-IPO matches in the IPO's three or four digit SIC. The final sample therefore consists of 462 IPO firms and 462 controls that matched in terms of industry and sales volume. Of the latter, 430 were matched within the four-digit SIC and the other 32 within the three-digit SIC.

STATISTICAL MODEL

A holding period return (HPR) was recorded for each IPO and the arithmetic mean of the HPRs for the IPO firms was compared with that of the controls. This process was repeated in calculating long-term HPR. The HPR is calculated as follows:

$$HPR = (e-b)/b.$$

Where e = ending stock price.
               b = beginning stock price.

HYPOTHESIS TESTING

IPOs versus similar non-IPO firms were tested for:

• Performance during the first day of trading.

• Performance during the first three years of trading.

Then the results were evaluated to detect any market anomalies during:

• Initial trading.

• Long-term performance.

FIRST DAY OF TRADING PERFORMANCE

Identify the IPOs from 1998–2000 and evaluate their performance versus the performance of similar non-IPO firms on their initial day of trading.

Hypothesis:

H_0: There is no significant difference between the mean first-day return of IPO companies and mean first-day return of similar non-IPO companies.

H_1: There is a significant difference between mean first-day return of IPO companies and mean first-day return of similar non-IPO companies.

What is needed to resolve this problem is to:

• Identify companies that had an IPO between January 1, 1998, and December 31, 2000.

• Identify companies that are similar in terms of size measured by annual sales and four-digit SIC that had an IPO during the same period but subsequently failed

• Obtain the opening stock price for each IPO and the closing price on the day the IPO occurred.

• Obtain the opening stock price and the closing price for each non-IPO firm analyzed.

If there is no matching firm within a particular IPO firm's four-digit SIC, a similar firm was chosen from the three-digit SIC. If no matching firms were found there, the IPO in question was deleted from the study. Other studies (Jan, 1997) matched firms within even two-digit SICs, but I felt the match had to be closer.

Data from *Investment Dealers'Digest Information Services* and the historical stock price database were entered directly to an Excel spreadsheet for further analysis. Once all the qualifying IPOs and their initial stock prices were input, the historical stock price database was used to determine the initial trading day closing price and the closing price three years later. This process was repeated for each stock.

The data from *Ward's Business Directory* was copied and transferred by hand to the same spreadsheet. Each IPO was matched with a company that had not had a successful stock offering during that year, was in the same industry, and was the closest match in terms of annual sales to the IPO being matched.

The HPR was calculated for each IPO on the day it went public. A t-test was used to compare the mean HPRs of the IPOs studied to the mean HPRs of the similar non-IPO studied. A significance level of 0.05 was used to test the null hypothesis. The t-test statistics for the difference in mean returns was calculated using the difference between the mean returns of the IPOs and the non-IPOs. The significance level of 0.05 was used to approximate the effects of commissions and taxes. The t-test was calculated manually and then re-tested using SPSS Statistical software.

FIRST THREE YEARS OF TRADING PERFORMANCE

The second problem is to evaluate the performance of the selected IPOs during their first three years of trading versus the performance of similar non-IPO firms.

Hypothesis:

H_0: There is no significant difference between the long-term mean return of IPO companies and the long-term mean return of similar non-IPO companies.

H_1: There is a significant difference between the long-term mean return of IPO companies and the long-term mean return of similar non-IPO companies.

To resolve the second problem it was necessary to:

- Obtain the opening stock price for each IPO on the day after the IPO and its closing price three years from that date.

- Obtain the opening stock price on the day after the IPO for each similar non-IPO firm studied and its closing price three years from that date.

The data from the World Wide Web were individually transferred directly to an Excel spreadsheet one stock at a time for further analysis. The HER for each IPO from the day after it went public to three years after that date was calculated. A t-test was used to compare the mean HPRs of the IPOs studied and the mean HPRs for the similar non-IPOs. The t-test was calculated manually and then re-tested using SPSS statistical software.

MARKET ANOMALIES: FIRST DAY OF TRADING

The third problem is to evaluate the results of the initial performance of the IPOs versus the similar non-IPO firms in order to detect any market anomalies as they relate to the efficient market hypothesis. For the purposes of this study there has not been a market anomaly if investors who acquire an IPO stock on the day it is issued do not experience abnormal rates of return compared to the similar non-IPO stocks. Testing of the Problem One hypothesis provides evidence for the possible existence of short-term anomalies in the IPO market.

The data needed to resolve the third problem are the results of the average HPRs calculated for the first problem found in the Excel spreadsheet used to calculate the HPRs.

The initial day mean HPRs for both types of firms were compared. A t-test significance level of 0.05 or greater could indicate a stock market anomaly. A significance level of 0.05 or less this would be in line with the efficient market hypothesis in that no abnormal returns could be derived from initial day trading in IPO companies.

MARKET ANOMALIES: LONG-TERM PERFORMANCE

The fourth problem is to evaluate the long-term performance of the IPOs versus the similar non-IPO firms to detect the existence of any market anomaly. Testing of the Problem Two hypothesis provides evidence for possible anomalies in the long-term IPO market.

The data needed to resolve the fourth problem are the results of the average HPRs calculated for the second problem, located on the Excel spreadsheet used to calculate the HPRs.

The data are treated by comparing the long-term mean HPRs for the two types of firms. A t-test significance level of 0.05 or greater could indicate a stock market anomaly in conflict with the efficient market hypothesis. A significance level of 0.05 or less would be in line with the efficient market hypothesis.

ANALYSIS AND FINDINGS

A quantitative approach was used for each problem to determine whether IPO companies underperform or overperform non-IPO peers both initially and over the long term.

FIRST DAY OF TRADING PERFORMANCE

A total of 462 IPO firms were identified. They were matched to 462 companies that had not had a recent IPO. The initial performance results for both types of firms is shown in Table A-1.

TABLE A-1
INITIAL PERFORMANCE OF IPO VERSUS NON-IPO FIRMS

	IPO Companies	Non-IPO Companies
Mean holding period return (HPR)	-4.26%	0.20%

It appears that on average the IPO companies studied underperformed non-IPO companies of similar size and industry, though not significantly. That is, IPO companies dropped in value from initial bid price to the close of the first day of trading. Table A-2 expands on the findings shown in Table A-1.

The t-test was performed using a significance level of 0.05. At this significance level, the difference between the two means lies within the acceptable region. Therefore, the null hypothesis that states the initial mean holding period returns would be the same is not rejected. Further testing showed that at a significance level of 0.10 or higher, the differ-

TABLE A-2
DIFFERENCE BETWEEN THE INITIAL MEANS: T-TEST RESULTS

	IPO Companies	Non-IPO Companies
Mean holding period return	-4.26%	0.20%
Standard deviation	0.5235	0.0468
Number of firms in study	462	462
Standard error of difference between the two means	0.0245	0.0245
Acceptable upper limit	0.048	0.048
Acceptable lower limit	-0.048	-0.048
Difference between the two means	-0.0446	-0.0446

ence between the two means would fall outside the acceptable level, indicating that the null hypothesis would not be true. This t-test shows that an investor who buys IPOs and then sells at the end of the initial day gets no abnormal returns. However, the significance level chosen was 0.05, and hence the null hypothesis cannot be rejected.

These findings are in conflict with older studies. For example, Garfinkel (1993), Eysell and Kummer (1993), Barry (1993), and others found initial underpricing of IPOs compared to similar non-IPOs or index benchmarks. All the studies mentioned measure initial day return using the opening day stock price. Studies using the subscription price rather than the opening price found initial IPO underpricing as well. Barry (1993) not only measured the initial day returns but also took first-day intraday measurements. He found all the initial IPO underpricing occurred during the first trading minutes of the day and that there were no abnormal returns for the remainder of the first day's trading.

In my opinion, IPOs are not always initially underpriced, especially during a three-year cycle, the term of this study. In addition, each of the studies mentioned were analyzing performance of IPOs issued in the 1980s. This study is observing more recent IPOs. The range of performance is shown in Table A-3.

TABLE A-3
NUMBER OF FIRMS INITIALLY PERFORMING POSITIVELY, NEGATIVELY, OR NO CHANGE

	IPO Companies	Non-IPO Companies
Initial positive performance	228	174
Initial negative performance	178	174
No initial price change	56	114

Table A-3 shows that although IPO firms initially underperformed non-IPOs, IPO firms with positive first-day performance outnumber non-IPO firms. This suggests that although more IPO firms initially outperformed non-IPO firms, those that underperformed, did so to a greater degree. Of the 462 IPOs studied, 76 in 1998, 212 in 1999, and 174 in 2000. Table A-4 indicates the year by year performance of both the IPOs and non-IPOs in this study.

TABLE A-4
INITIAL PERFORMANCE OF IPOs VERSUS NON-IPO FIRMS BY YEAR

	IPO Companies	Non-IPO Companies
1998 mean HPR	-3.99%	0.45%
1999 mean HPR	-3.12%	0.07%
2000 mean HPR	-4.72%	-0.11%

Table A-4 shows that the initial performance for IPO companies as well as non-IPO companies was weakest in 2000. In all three years studied, the initial trading day mean return for IPO companies was not only negative it below that of the non-IPO companies. (It should be noted that in 2000 far fewer companies had IPOs than in the other two years.)

FIRST THREE YEARS OF TRADING PERFORMANCE

The second problem is to evaluate the performance of IPOs versus similar non-IPO firms during their first three years of trading. The period is measured from the opening price of all companies on the day after each IPO issued to the closing price on the same date three years later.

Table A-5 shows three-year performance as measured by the mean HPR for each sample.

TABLE A-5
Long-Term Performance of IPO Versus Non-IPO Firms

	IPO Companies	Non-IPO Companies
Mean holding period return (annualized)	19.59%	23.85%

IPO companies were underperformed compared to their counter-parts during the three-year period, but not significantly. The return for an investor in IPO companies over this time frame would have been only about 82 percent of the return that would have been earned in similar non-IPO companies.

Table A-6 compares performance on a variety of measures.

TABLE A-6
DIFFERENCE BETWEEN THE LONG-TERM MEANS: T-TEST RESULTS

	IPO Companies	Non-IPO Companies
Mean holding period return	58.78%	71.56%
Standard deviation	1.84	1.65
Number of firms in study	462	462
Standard error of difference between the two means	0.115	0.115
Acceptable upperlimit	0.2256	0.2256
Acceptable lower limit	-0.2256	-0.2256
Difference between the two means	-0.1278	-0.1278

The t-test was performed using a significance level of 0.05. The results show that the difference between mean holding period returns for the two types of companies was within the region of acceptability for this study. Therefore, the null hypothesis that the two long-term sample means are equal within a 5 percent region of acceptability holds true. There are no abnormal long-term benefits to investing in IPOs. In fact, investing in IPOs for the three years after the initial trading day would yield a lower return than investing in the similar non-IPO companies. I believe this is mainly due to the use of a balanced scorecard approach to the IPOs.

Table A-7 shows a year-by-year breakdown of the long term performance of companies in this study.

TABLE A-7
LONG-TERM PERFORMANCE OF IPO VERSUS NON-IPO FIRMS
BY YEAR OF ISSUANCE (ANNUALIZED)

	IPO Companies	Non-IPO Companies
Mean HPR for 1998 issues	17.66%	21.75%
Mean HPR for 1999 issue	19.66%	26.13%
Mean HPR for 2000 issues	23.12%	25.84%

In each year studied IPO performance was inferior to non-IPO performance over the following three years. Companies that issued IPOs in 1998 fared worse than those that had IPOs in 1999 and 2000. Although far fewer companies issued IPOs in 2000 than in 1998 or 1999, the long-term performance of the IPO firms issued in 2000 was superior to that of 1998 and 1999. This is possibly because the market was flooded with IPOs in 2000 compared with 1998 and 1999. Again, this researcher believes that once again this is showing increased awareness of the balanced scorecard ramification on the IPOs during 2000.

MARKET ANOMALIES: FIRST DAY OF TRADING

The third problem was to evaluate the results of the initial performance of the IPOs against the performance of the matched firms in order to see whether there was any market anomaly. An anomaly would be evident if an investor could on average consistently earn abnormal returns, after adjusting for the effects of commissions and taxes. For this problem the investment period was from initial bid price to first-day closing price.

A t-test for the difference between the mean HPRs of the two types of companies was performed using a significance level of 0.05 (representing the effects of taxes and commissions). The results show that both means lie within the acceptable area, which confirms the null hypothesis. No market anomaly was detected because there is not a significant difference between the IPO firms and the non-IPO firms that would allow for abnormal returns. The t-test was repeated using SPSS Statistical software and the results were confirmed.

MARKET ANOMALIES: LONG-TERM PERFORMANCE

The fourth problem was to compare long-term performance of the two types of companies firms in order to see if there was any market anomaly related to the efficient market hypothesis. An anomaly would be present if an investor could on average consistently earn abnormal returns after adjusting for the effects of commission and taxes. For this problem the performance period for all companies was from the starting price the day after the IPO to exactly three years later.

A t-test for the difference between the IPO companies and the non-IPO companies long-term mean HPRs was performed using a significance level of 0.05 to represent the effects of taxes and commissions. The results show that the two means lie within the acceptance area, which confirms the null hypothesis. There is no market anomaly because there is not a significant difference between the IPO firms and the matched firms that would allow for abnormal returns. The t-test was repeated using SPSS Statistical software and the results were confirmed.

IPO EARNINGS SURPRISES

Consistent earnings surprises in any direction could contain a message about the inherent financial abilities of a company. The following identifies the specific characteristics of those firms that perform well and those that perform badly in the market place and should assist you in evaluating your own situation.

Earnings surprises stem from forecast errors. As part of their work of projecting earnings estimates, financial analysts evaluate financial ratios. Discrepancies in these ratios and the resulting evaluations could cause problems in estimating the true value of a company and therefore lead to an earnings surprise.

Inefficient can have important implications for the efficiency of pricing in securities markets. If they take this study's results into consideration when constructing their portfolios, investors will be better informed about the performance potential of their portfolios. All investors should therefore pay close attention to these results when making such investment decisions

The purpose of this study is to identify the financial characteristics of U.S. publicly traded firms that have produced consistently positive and consistently negative earnings surprises in the 10-year period between 1989 and 1998, and to analyze the relationship between these financial characteristics and the market's interpretations of the financial statements of these firms.

Finance theory asserts that the return associated with an investment is consistent with its risk. This leads us to the conventional wisdom in finance about efficient. Stock markets, in general, are semi-efficient. That is, security prices adjust rapidly to the arrival of new information, and arbitrage opportunities are, at best, extremely rare and short-lived.

Yet contradictory to this conventional wisdom, it has also been found that publicly available financial statement numbers can predict future abnormal returns for U.S. stocks. These findings seriously challenged the theory that the market processes public information efficiently and thus encouraged fundamental analysis.

I thought it necessary to look at earnings surprises to find out what might create an earnings surprise, such a surprise occurring whenever earnings are inconsistent with the consensus estimates of analysts. The goal was to identify two distinct sets of firm characteristics that have led to either consistently positive or consistently negative earnings surprises.

EARNINGS SURPRISES IN GENERAL

Researchers have reported that certain financial characteristics of firms in the restaurant industry may be used to predict whether a given restaurant company is a good investment risk. Therefore indicating that risk is indeed significantly related to financial characteristics. While these results cannot be used to draw inferences about all firms and abnormal earnings behavior, they are useful in identifying what firm-specific characteristics to look for. Indeed, if risk is significantly related to certain financial characteristics, so may be abnormal earnings.

In addition, some studies have also found that financial statement analysis can provide useful information about the relationship between risk and return by effectively identifying the market's inefficient use of financial statement information.

In these studies, financial statements for each firm in each group were evaluated on a historical basis (ratio analysis). Then relationships between these ratios and the abnormal earnings of each firm were determined. The goal is to identify the characteristics of publicly traded companies that have consistent earnings surprises over time, and to provide insight into the market's use of financial statements from an earnings perspective.

Henry Latane and Charles Jones (1997) hypothesized that unexpected information (such as an earnings surprise) and the accompanying revision of probability beliefs will have a measurable effect on stock prices. They attempted to measure how the information in quarterly earnings reports affected stock prices. They concluded that excess holding period returns (HPRs) are significantly related to unexpected earnings and that the adjustment to unexpected earnings is relatively slow, probably because the unexpected earnings themselves are serially correlated.

Some researchers state that in finance, the phrase "forecast inefficiency" is defined as forecasts that fail to accurately incorporate new information on a timely basis or that are biased. Such forecasts have also been described as irrational or suboptimal. In addition, previous studies that report inefficiency in analysts' forecasts, find that they are upwardly biased and inaccurately reflect the information available. Some studies conclude that analysts under react to information, others that they overreact.

If markets treat analysts' forecasts as both rational and statistically optimal, then inefficient forecasts could have important implications for the efficiency of pricing in securities markets. The apparent tendency of analysts to misinterpret earnings information in an attempt to discriminate between the following three hypotheses were reexamined:

1. Analysts systematically under react to new earnings information.

2. Analysts systematically overreact to new earnings information.

3. Analysts are systematically optimistic in their reactions.

The forecasts studied provided evidence that analysts (1) make biased forecasts and (2) misinterpret the impact of new information, and that the bias tends to be upward, a challenge to the efficient market theory.

Some researched have cited a number of papers that had recently examined stock returns and suggested that investors in general, and analysts in particular, err in making forecasts of future stock prices and earnings by irrationally extrapolating recent price and earnings information. Specifically, when analysts and investors observe abnormal earnings and price performance over a brief period, they erroneously project that these trends will continue.

My own study described here found evidence consistent with this in that it shows, by constructing two groups of rims with consistent positive and negative available financial statement information, that such under- and over-reactions are inconsistent with rational forecasts and efficient market hypothesis. The study found a statistically significant relationship between financial ratios (firm characteristics) and earnings surprise events (firm performance). The implication is that analysts, when assessing and estimating potential earnings, misinterpret the financial characterizes and therefore miscalculate a firm's actual earnings potential, preparing the way for earnings surprises.

In other research, the profitability of a trading strategy based on information from company financial statements was investigated. Specifically, a summary measure of the current year's financial statement information, labeled Pr, that indicated the likelihood of positive one-year-ahead earnings changes was constructed. The trading strategy they used was to take long positions in companies that were forecast to have a high probability of a future earnings increase, and short positions in companies expected to have a low probability of a future earnings increase.

For all stocks, regardless of their calendar year, the strategy earned cumulative market-adjusted returns of 14.53 percent over a two-year holding period and 20.83 percent over three years. Adjusted for size, the returns were 9.08 percent and 11.85 percent.

Two approaches to address the value of fundamental analysis has also been used. The first mirrored the research described above. The second was a more direct approach that marked any type of potential source of risk and commented on relative strengths. Analysis was extended to whether financial distress and takeovers might have provided alternative explanations for the results. Applied to stock prices, this approach found that an investor could have used public financial statement information to earn abnormal returns using a strategy of predicting one-year-ahead earnings changes.

Two extreme approaches to using financial statement numbers to predict the effect of future earnings on stock returns were identified. The first was exclusively on existing theory concerning the linkages between accounting numbers and firm valuation. As an example, a popular method of financial statement analysis using financial ratios that measure the following four characteristics (1) profitability, (2) turnover, (3) liquidity, and (4) gearing. In addition, a more practical approach aimed at explaining contemporaneous abnormal returns using financial variables that include 12 fundamental signals identified from various sources, including professional journals and commentaries and security firm newsletters was also adopted. This second approach allowed the choice of indicators to emerge from the analysis—to let the data decide.

This approach asserted that in predicting stock returns, the problem is not in determining whether one stock has a higher value than another but is identifying stocks that the market currently overvalues or undervalues but will correctly value by the end of the holding period for calculating returns.

In applying the previous study, it was concluded that an investor could have earned abnormal returns by exploiting published financial information to predict future earnings changes. The conclusion that an investor could use this kind of information mechanically, was applied uniformly across companies, to predict subsequent-year earnings changes and to systematically earn abnormal investment returns.

The objective of my own study is to identify two groups of firms that the market consistently overvalued (poor performers) or undervalued (good performers). Financial characteristics specific to each group are then documented as guidelines for future trading and investment.

DATA AND SAMPLE DESCRIPTION

Earnings surprises are defined as company-reported quarterly earnings that are above or below the consensus estimates of analysts. Earnings surprise data is obtained from the Zack database (6,000-plus firms) and financial statement information from the Compustat database. Quarterly earnings surprises are reported from 1989 to 1998 for 2,760 firms.

In this study, I chose from the original 2,760 sample firms only those that have had earnings surprises, positive or negative, at least 40 percent of the time during the 40-quarter period under study. The purpose is to find firms that consistently deviated from the consensus estimates in one direction or another.

The sample firms were then separated into two groups based on the size and direction of the earnings surprises. Good performers are firms that reported positive quarterly earnings surprises of 5 percent or more at least 70 percent of the time. Poor performers are those firms that reported negative quarterly earnings surprises of 5 percent or more at least 60 percent of the time over the 40-quarter period (the 60 percent ratio is used because 70 percent produced a very small sample). The sample thus consists of 86 good performers and 76 poor performers.

The ratios shown in the tables were constructed from analysis of company financial information—current ratio, debt ratio, debt to equity ratio, cash flow to total assets, return on assets, return on equity, research and development expenditures to total sales, market to book ratio, net profit margin, and gross profit margin.

Table B-1 (pages 168–169) reports the names and ticker symbols for all the firms in both subsamples. Table B-2 (page 170) reports summary statistics on financial ratio for each subsample. Maximums, minimums, medians, averages, and standard deviations for total assets, total revenue, net income, stock price, book value, and EPS for each group are reported in Table B-3 (page 171). Table B-4 (page 171) shows the number of years since each firm went public (age) and the industries to which they belong.

EMPIRICAL FINDINGS

In summarizing the ratios and related data displayed in the tables, this research follows the convention of reporting median values because of the skewing properties of accounting ratios.

In both groups total revenues and total assets are on average below $200 million and book values below $70 million. In general, then, we are analyzing micro-capitalization firms (see Table B-3). Moreover, in both groups the firms come from a multitude of industries (Table B-4).

There is a distinct relationship between size, market-to-book ratios, and returns on securities. It can therefore be concluded that size and market-to-book ratios for financial and no-financial firms have similar meanings in that respect. It has also been concluded that size and market-to-book premium did not differ significantly between financial and non-financial firms, so these two groups can justifiably be compared with each other. However, within these two groups, there are some distinct differences with respect to financial characteristics.

Summary statistics on financial ratios for each subsample are reported in Table B-2. The market-to-book ratios are 1.59 for poor performers and 2.64 for good performers. Although not too far apart, these numbers indicate that market participants are assigning a higher market value to good performers than to poor performers. As a general rule, the values that markets assign to firms are based on expectations of the growth opportunities of those firms.

The current ratio is a liquidity ratio. Liquidity is the ability of an asset to be converted to cash quickly at low cost. The current ratio is the ratio of current assets to current liabilities—the number of dollars in current assets for every dollar in current liability. Current assets are those immediately convertible to cash and current liabilities are those payable within a year.

Poor performers in this study have a current ratio of 2 and good performers have a current ratio of 2.53. Although good performers have more dollars in current assets for each dollar in current liabilities, the poor performers trail the good ones closely, so it could not be established clearly that one group is superior over the other based upon this criteria alone.

Gross profit margin, a measure of operating performance, is calculated by dividing operating income by sales. Operating income is income before depreciation, interest, and taxes. Poor performers have 9 cents in operating income per dollar of sales, and good performers have 12 cents. Thus, good performers are noticeably, if not greatly, advantaged in this aspect.

Net profit margin is the ratio of net income to sales. Here, for every dollar of sales, poor performers have 1 cent in net income and performers have 4 cents. Net profit margin for good performers is thus considerably higher.

The R&D to sales ratio is important in the sense that it shows how concerned a firm is about its future, the relevance of its product, and its competitive position in the market place. Here again the good performers exhibit a distinguished difference. They spend 12 cents of every sales dollar on R&D vs. only 5 cents spent by poor performers.

Cash flow to total assets is calculated by dividing operating income before depreciation by total assets. It indicates how much cash flow is generated for every dollar in assets held. This ratio indicates the return on investment the firm is earning. In other words, how effectively assets are being put to use. Again, the difference between the two groups is noticeable—9 cents in cash flow generated per dollar in assets for poor performers versus 14 cents for good performers.

Return on assets (ROA) is a profitability ratio that is often used to measure the performance of a firm. It is calculated by dividing earnings before interest and taxes (EBIT) by total assets. Notably, the ROA for poor performers is 1 percent and for good performers it is 6 percent, a considerably superior performance.

Return on equity (ROE), another measure of profitability, looks at return on shareholders' equity. It is calculated by dividing earnings available by common stock equity. Here the results are even more definitive. An ROE of 2 percent for poor performers versus 11.5 percent for good performers.

The debt ratio shows the amount of dollars in total debt for every dollar in total assets. In other words, it shows what percentage of the firm's total capitalization is short and long-term debt. For poor performers, the debt ratio is 25 percent, more than double the 12 percent for good performers. This is another clear difference between the two groups, and another considerable advantage for the good performers.

Finally, the debt to equity ratio measures the proportion of total debt to total equity. This tells us how many dollars a company has in total debt for every dollar in total equity. For the good performers the debt to equity ratio is 15 percent. For the poor performers it is an enormous 41 percent, almost three times as much. This means that poor performers must allocate a much larger portion of their operating income to debt service. It would also be one of the contributing factors to the lower net income of poor performers.

The filtered 162-firm sample in this study turned out to include very low-capitalization firms. For these, the results showed a relationship between company financial characteristics (financial statement data) and company performance (consistent with positive or negative earning surprises).

The results (see Table B-2), clearly indicate that good performers have very different, and far superior, financial characteristics than poor performers. The relationship between financial characteristics (financial ratios) and performance as indicated by consistent positive or negative earnings surprises is clear. The set of financial ratios characteristic of good performers is quite distinct from the set of ratios characteristic of poor performers. For this sample, that relationship would indicate that when analysts assess the potential earnings of a firm, in regularly misinterpreting a firm's financial characteristics, they thereby miscalculate the firm's earnings potential, paving the way for an earnings surprise.

In general, major brokerage houses do not follow micro capitalizations. Very few analysts follow these firms, which are usually referred to as "undiscovered by the street." This could also explain to an extent why these firms consistently reported earnings surprises.

Empirical research data has previously identified a number of firm-specific variables that are correlated with analyst earnings forecast errors. These include the size of the firm and the number of analysts following the firm. It can be concluded from these that average earnings forecast error (FE) and average absolute forecast error (ABSFE) are negatively and significantly correlated with the number of financial analysts following each firm (EST) and the market value of its equity (SIZE), which proxy for the information environment of a firm. The intuition is that large firms are followed more by the media and by analysts, ensuring broader and more timely dissemination of news about them.

These facts may explain the consistent variations that exist between the announced earnings of firms in the sample and the consensus estimates of their earnings. For the sample firms, even considering they are not widely covered, those few analysts that do follow these firms are still misinterpreting the financial characteristics and miscalculating actual earnings potentials.

This research indicates that information that is publicly available in the form of financial statements (financial ratios). can indeed point to the potential performance and earnings behavior of particular firms. In other words, in the context of this data set, the two distinct sets of financial ratios that have proved to be specific to good versus poor performers (Table B-2) can also be used to predict which firms will be good and poor performers.

Excess HPRs, as has been shown, are very significantly related to unexpected earnings and adjustment to unexpected earnings performance is relatively slow, probably because the unexpected earnings themselves are significantly serially correlated. It is also known that HPR is directly related to a firm's value. Consequently, if excess HPRs are significantly related to unexpected earnings, the values of respondent firms do not reflect the publicly available financial data. These constant surprises thus inform the reader that markets are unable to perceive true potential performance and therefore err in valuing these firms.

If markets treat the forecasts of analysts as both rational and statistically optimal, the fact that the forecasts are actually inefficient could have important implications for the efficiency of pricing in securities markets. Systematic under- or overreaction to information can thus be perceived as inconsistent with rational forecasts and with an efficient market for expert information.

If for any reason markets and analysts fail to recognize and accurately interpret financial statement data as they pertain to the earnings potentials of particular firms, it would be possible for an investor to gain an advantage by buying good performers and shorting poor performers, thus making a superior risk-adjusted return. This situation would certainly render markets inefficient in this particular sense.

CONCLUSIONS

The results of this research into earnings surprises and their relation to financial statement data show a relationship between the two. The results also suggest that financial analysts systematically under- or overreact to publicly available information (financial statement data), thus making their forecast earnings inefficiently and setting the stage for consistent earnings surprises. The research additionally concludes that inefficient forecasts have potentially important implications for the efficiency of pricing in the securities market.

Companies like Microsoft, General Electric, and Cisco have changed the old market standards. Total market capitalization for these three firms together surpasses $1.5 trillion. Multibillion-dollar firms are now considered small capitalization firms.

Today's capital markets are changing fast to adjust to the information technology revolution. When Internet companies first appeared, dozens of new firms were going public every day, commanding billion-dollar capitalizations, selling like hot cakes, with kids trading in them on personal computers. Many of these same kids were among those who lost all they owned because they were unaware of the intrinsic inefficiencies and were uninformed of the balanced scorecard and the other intangibles that go into making a firm successful.

It is no wonder $200 million dollar firms are virtually being ignored now. Excessive sudden wealth and participation took the markets by surprise. Investment banking firms and competent analysts found they were too busy for firms with market capitalization of less than a few billion dollars.

This situation raises numerous questions.

1. Are markets becoming less efficient?

2. Is it time for investors to start scrutinizing the suddenly ignored smaller firms in search of common characteristics that could turn the odds in their favor?

The results of this research seem to indicate that this might be a good idea. The study has also provided new guidelines for analyzing an investment, in the form of distinct sets of financial ratios specific to potential good or poor-performers.

By carefully selecting firms according to these guidelines, prudent investors might enhance their portfolios and get more for their investment money. A higher return for the same risk may be very possible.

Analysts and investors might use these guidelines to reappraise their estimates on earnings and change the make-up of their portfolios to emphasize the better performers. Future studies, however, may shed more light on the measurement aspects of these issues.

TABLE B-1
POOR PERFORMERS

Name	Market Ref.	Name	Market Ref.
Agnico Eagle.	AME	Intergraph.	INGR
Argosy Gaming.	AGY	IntegraVision	INVI
Angeion Corp	ANGN	It Group Inc	ITX
Borden Chem/Pla	BCU	Jacobson Stores	JCBS
Birmingham Steel	BIR	Kcs Energy Inc	KCS
Basin Expl Inc.	BSNX	Key Tronic.	KTCC
Coeur Dalene Mi	CDE	Key Technology	KTEC
Chieftain Int'l.	CID	Ligand Pharma-B	LGND
Celadon Group	CLDN	Molecir Bio-Sys	MB
Cominco Ltd	CLT	Metrocall Inc	MCLL
Coho Energy Inc.	COHOC	Metromedia Int	MMG
Coram Hlthcare	CRH	Marine Transprt	MTLX
Century Comms A	CTYA	Midwest Grain	MWGP
Converse-Del	CVE	Noble Affiliate	NBL
Digital Biometr	DBII	Netrix Corp	NTRX
Deb Shops	DEBS	Odwalla Inc	ODWA
Dynamic Hc Tech	DHTI	Overseas Shipho	OSG
Trump Htl & Cas	DJT	Ranger Oil Ltd	RGO
Deltaware Tech	DWTI	Ross Systems	ROSS
Echo Bay Mines	ECO	Sheldahl	SHEL
Eagle Food Ctrs	EGLEQ	Safety-Kleen	SK
Entrade Inc	ETA	Simula Inc	SMU
Fairchild Corp	FA	Sonic Solutions	SNIC
Frontier Oil	FTO	Stanford Teleco	STII
Grubb & Ellis	GBE	Stone Weber	SW
Gardenburger	GBUR	3d Systems Corp	TDSC
Gulf Cda Res	GOU	Thor Inds Inc	THO
Geoworks Corp.	GWRX	Thomaston Mills	TMSTA
Sports Supp Grp	GYM	Tokheim Corp	TOK
High Plains Cp	HIPC	Tower Air Inc	TORQ
Intermedia Comm	ICIX	Triarc Cos Cl A	TRY
Indentix Inc.	IDX	Thermo Terratec	TTT
Igen Intl.	IGEN	Ultralife Battle	UWR
Insteel Inds.	III	Worldtex Inc	WTX
Imclone Systems	IMCL	Young Brdcast-A	YBTVA
Intermagnetics	IMG	Venator Group	Z
Imperial Oil Lt	IMO	Zenith Natl Ins	ZNT

TABLE B-1
GOOD PERFORMERS (CONT.)

Name	Market Ref.	Name	Market Ref.
Airtan Hldgs	AAIR	Merrill Corp	MRLL
Abr Info Svcs	ABRX	Medicis Pharm-A.	MRX
Amcol Intl Cp	ACO	Micro Warehouse	MWHS
Amer Eagle ouff	AEOS	Northwest Air	NSIT
Anadigics Corp	ANAD	Protein Design	PDLI
Appld Science	ASTX	Periphonics Cp	PERI
Avt Corp	AVTC	Playboy Entrp-B	PLA
Biocryst Pharm	BCRX	Polymedica Corp	PLMD
Biggs & Stratt	BGG	Pmc-Sierra Inc	PMCS
Conti Airls-B	CAL	Scp Pool Corp	POOL
Cdw Comptr Ctrs.	CDWC	Premisys Commun	PRMS
Cfw Comms Co	CFWC	Proxim Inc	PROX
Chicos Fas Fnc	CHCS	Project Softwre	PSDI
Comair Hldgs	COMR	Peoplesoft Inc	PSFT
Cree Inc	CREE	Pac Sunwear Cal.	PSUN
Digital Link Cp	DLNK	Paine Webber G	PWJ
Dendrite Int	KRTE	Quickturn Dsgn	QKTN
Devon Energy	DVN	Qlogic Corp	QLGC
Eagle Hardware	EAGL	Rational Softwr	RATL
Elcor Corp	ELK	Resmed Inc	RMD
Epimmune Inc	EPMN	Remedy Corp	RMDY
Ezenia Inc	EZEN	Romac Intl Inc	KFRC
Freept Mc Cop-B	FCX	Reliance Steel	RS
Fossil Inc	FOSL	Sli Inc	SLI
Gadzooks Inc	GADZ	Semitool Inc	SMTL
Genesco Inc	GCO	Simpson Mfg Inc	SSD
Gilead Sciences	GILD	Software Spectr.	SSPE
Hispanic Bdcst	HBCCA	Stanley Furn Co	STLY
Herbalife Int-A	HARBA	Timerland Co A	TBL
Harmonic Inc.	HLIT	Three-Five Sys	TFS
Hnc Software	HNCS	Technitrol Inc	TNL
Kerr-Mcgee	KMG	TV Guide Inc	TVGIA
Lehman Bros Hld	LEH	Transwitch Corp	TXCC
Landamerica Fin	LFG	Uromed Corp	URMD
Legato Systems	LGTO	Viasoft Inc	VIAS
Mdc Hldgs	MDC	Vical Inc	VICL
Mercury Interac	MERQ	Veritas Software	VRTS
M/I Schot Homes.	MHO	Wall Data Inc	WALL
Monaco Coach Cp	MNC	Wang Labs New	WANG
Mitchell Engy-B	MND.B	World Access	WAXS
Modtech Hldgs	MODT	Mem Elec Matrl	WFR
Modis Prof Svcs	MPS	Winsloew Furn	WLFI

TABLE B-2
OVERALL RATIOS

Description	Median	Average	Standard Deviation
Poor Performers			
Current ratio	1.99	2.90	2.92
Operating income. before depreciation to total assets	0.09	0.04	0.23
Profit margin	0.01	-0.33	3.01
Gross profit margin	0.09	-0.27	2.95
Return on assets	0.01	-0.03	0.47
Return on equity	0.02	-0.08	2.52
Market-to-book value	1.59	1.59	25.16
Debt ratio	0.25	0.29	0.25
Debt to equity	0.41	1.01	6.38
R&D to sales	0.05	0.83	5.02
Good Performers			
Current ratio	2.53	3.94	4.85
Operating income before depreciation to total assets	0.14	0.12	0.17
Profit margin	0.04	-0.40	3.66
Gross profit margin	0.12	-0.30	3.37
Return on assets	0.06	0.02	0.17
Return on equity	0.115	0.10	1.34
Market-to-book value	2.64	3.62	6.69
Debt ratio	0.12	0.19	0.22
Debt to equity	0.15	0.57	18.34
R&D to sales	0.12	0.73	2.90

TABLE B-3
FIRM SIZE DATA
(Amounts in millions, except Standard Deviation.)

	Maximum	Minimum	Median	Standard Average	Deviation
Poor Performers					
Total revenue	9,962	0.078	180,921	500	1,356.918
Total assets	13,451	0.786	176,317	649	1,400.736
Book value	6,421	-725.252	68.727	234	646.037
Net income	593	-495.000	0.925	-1.305	78.200
Earnings per share	11	-41.667	0.065	-0.173	2.472
Stock price	64	0.547	9.875	12.278	9.311
Good Performers					
Total revenue	19,894	0.270	139,547	754	2,037.965
Total assets	153,890	2.816	119.285	2,382	13,492.612
Book value	4,505	-3,865	60,127	152	529.228
Net income	2,602	-2,343	6.174	17.725	177.736
Earnings per share	144.348	-57.082	0.654	0.723	6.728
Stock price	120.250	0.250	17.250	21.226	15.567

TABLE B-4
INDUSTRIES AND AGES

Industries	Percent of Total	Industries	Percent of Total
Poor Performers:		*Good Performers:*	
Percent <10 years public, 34%		*Percent <10 years public, 66%*	
Crude oil/service	10%	Prepackaged software	15%
Systems design	6%	Semiconductor	9%
Prepackaged software	6%	Computer comm.Equipment	2%
Hazardous waste	4%	Air transport	5%
Special industry machinery	4%	Clothing	5%
Gold/silver ores	2%	Biological diagnostics	5%
Miscellaneous industries	68%	Pharmaceuticals	4%
		Securities/brokers	3%
		Printing	2%
		Miscellaneous industries	50%

SAMPLE AGREEMENT FOR UNDERWRITING SHARES OF A COMPANY

THIS AGREEMENT made at _____ on this _____ of 200X, between _____ Ltd., a company incorporated under the Companies Act, 1956, and having its registered office at _____ ("the company"), which expression shall be deemed to include its successors and assigns) and M/s. PDQ, a partnership registered under the Partnership Act, 1932 and having its place of business at _____ ("the underwriters"), which expression shall be deemed to include every partner for the time being of the said firm, the survivor or survivors, or the legal representatives, executors or administrators of the last partner.

WHEREAS the company proposes to issue _____ equity shares and offer the same for public subscription at $_____ per share in accordance with the terms of the draft prospectus, a copy of which is annexed hereto, or with such modifications therein as may be mutually agreed upon between the company and the underwriters.

AND WHEREAS the underwriters have agreed to underwrite the subscription of these shares on the terms and conditions hereinafter appearing, The Company and the Underwriters agree as follows:

1. The company shall issue _____ equity shares at $_____ each for public subscription in terms of the draft prospectus, on or before the _____ day of _____ 200X, or such later date as shall be mutually agreed upon but not after the _____ day of _____ 200X.

2. The underwriters shall on or before the closing of the subscription list apply for _____ shares or cause the same to be applied for by responsible persons, who shall pay on application the moneys payable on the number of shares applied for by them and who shall not withdraw their applications before notification of allotment of shares to them.

3. If on the closing of the list under the prospectus the _____ shares have been allotted on applications received from the public, the responsibility of the underwriters will cease and no allotment is to be made to the underwriters under this agreement; but if said _____ shares is not allotted to the public, but any smaller number of such shares is so allotted, the underwriters undertake to stand for the difference between the said _____ shares and the number of the shares allotted to the public and company may allot to the underwriters the number of shares that have not been applied for by such members of the public or such responsible persons as aforesaid and the underwriters shall accept the shares so allotted and pay all application and allotment money in respect of those shares in accordance with the prospectus.

4. The underwriters irrevocably authorize the company to apply the said _____ shares or any part thereof in the name and on behalf of the underwriters in accordance with the terms of the prospectus and authorize the directors of the company to allot the said _____ shares of the company or part thereof to the underwriters; in the event of the company making an application for such shares in the names of the underwriters, the underwriters shall hold the company harmless and indemnified in respect of such application.

5. The company shall pay to the underwriters in cash a commission of _____ percent on the nominal value of the shares within _____ days from the allotment of the said _____ shares; but should an allotment of the shares be made to the underwriters in accordance with the terms of this agreement, the commission shall not be payable until the underwriters pay the application and allotment moneys payable in respect of all the shares allotted to the underwriters.

6. Time is the essence of this agreement.

7. This agreement shall be executed in duplicate, with the original retained by the company and the duplicate by the underwriters.

IN WITNESS WHEREOF the parties have signed this agreement on the date ascribed.

Signed and delivered by _____
named company by its President:

_____

Signed and delivered by M/s. ABC, the underwriters by the Managing Partner:

_____

WITNESSES:
1. _____

_____

_____

2. _____

_____

_____

STATEMENT OF POLICY— SMALL COMPANY OFFERING REGISTRATION (SCOR)

ADOPTED APRIL 28, 1996

I. INTRODUCTION

The following guidelines of the North American Securities Administrators Association, Inc. (NASAA) provide for the uniform treatment of registrations of small company offerings which are exempt from federal registration under Rule 504 of Regulation D, Regulation A, or Section 3(a)(11) of the Securities Act of 1933, and are consistent with public investor protection and in the public interest. The Securities Administrator ("Administrator") may waive any standard set forth in this Policy Statement and may also impose substantive standards not contained in this Policy Statement.

II. APPLICATION

The requirements contained in this Policy Statement shall apply to registrations that utilize Registration Form U-7 and are exempt from federal registration under (1) Rule 504 of Regulation D, (2) Regulation A, or (3) Section 3(a)(11).

III. REQUIREMENTS FOR QUALIFICATION TO USE SCOR

Registrations covered in this Policy Statement shall meet the following requirements:

A. The issuer shall:

1) be a corporation or centrally managed limited liability company organized under the law of the United States or Canada, or any state, province, or territory or possession thereof, or the District of Columbia, and have its principal place of business in one of the foregoing;

2) not be subject to the reporting requirements of Section 13 or 15(d) of the Securities Exchange Act of 1934;

3) not be an investment company registered or required to be registered under the Investment Company Act of 1940;

4) not be engaged in or propose to be engaged in petroleum exploration and production, mining, or other extractive industries;

5) not be a development stage company that either has no specific business plan or purpose or has indicated that its business plan is to engage in merger or acquisition with an unidentified company or companies or other entity or person; and

6) not be disqualified under Section IV of this Policy Statement.

B. The offering price for common stock or common ownership interests (hereinafter, collectively referred to as common stock), the exercise price for options, warrants, or rights to common stock, or the conversion price for securities convertible into common stock, must be greater or equal to US - $1.00 per share or unit of interest. The issuer must agree with the Administrator that is will not split its common stock, or declare a stock dividend for two years after the effective date of the registration if such action has the effect of lowering the price below US $1.00.

C. Commissions, fees, or other remuneration for soliciting any prospective purchaser in connection with the offering in the state are only paid to persons who, if required to be registered or licensed, the issuer believes, and has reason to believe, are appropriately registered or licensed in the state.

D. Financial statements shall be prepared in accordance with either US or Canadian generally accepted accounting principles. If appropriate, a reconciliation note should be provided. If the Company has not conducted significant operations, statements of receipts and disbursements shall be included in lieu of statements of income. Interim financial statements may be unaudited. All other financial statements shall be audited by independent certified public accountants, provided, however, that if each of the following four conditions are met, such financial statements in lieu of being audited may be reviewed by independent certified public accountants in accordance with the Accounting and Review Service Standards promulgated by the American Institute of Certified Public Accountants or the Canadian equivalent;

1) the Company shall not have previously sold securities through an offering involving the general solicitation of prospective investors by means of advertising, mass mailing, public meetings, "cold call" telephone solicitation, or any other method directed toward the public;

2) the Company has not been previously required under federal, state, provincial or territorial securities laws to provide audited financial statements in connection with any sale of its securities;

3) the aggregate amount of all previous sales of securities by the Company (exclusive of debt financing with banks and similar commercial lenders) shall not exceed US $1,000,000; and

4) the amount of the present offering does not exceed US $1,000,000.

E. The offering shall be made in compliance with Rule 504 of Regulation D, Regulation A, or Section 3(a)(11) of the Securities Act of 1933.

F. The issuer shall comply with the General Instructions to SCOR in Part I of the NASAASCOR Issuer's Manual.

IV. DISQUALIFICATIONS

A. Unless the Administrator determines that it is not necessary under the circumstances that the disqualification under this section be applied, application for registrations referred to in Section II shall be denied if the issuer, any of its officers, directors, ten percent or greater stockholders, promoters, or selling agents or, any officer, director or partner of any selling agent:

1) has filed an application for registration which is subject to a currently effective stop order entered pursuant to any state or provincial securities laws within five years prior to the filing of the registration statement;

2) has been convicted, within five years prior to the filing of the current application for registration, of any felony involving fraud or deceit, including, but not limited to, forgery, embezzlement, obtaining money under false pretenses, larceny, or conspiracy to defraud;

3) is currently subject to any state or provincial administrative enforcement order or judgment entered by that state's or province's securities administrator within five years prior to the filing of the current application for registration;

4) is subject to any state or provincial administrative enforcement order or judgment in which fraud or deceit, including, but not limited to, making untrue statements of material facts and omitting to state material facts, was found, and the order or judgment was entered within five years prior to the filing of the current application for registration;

5) is subject to any state or provincial administrative enforcement order or judgment which prohibits, denies, or revokes the use of any exemption from registration in connection with the offer, purchase, or sale of securities;

6) is currently subject to any order, judgment, or decree of any court of competent jurisdiction that temporarily, preliminarily, or permanently restrains or enjoins such party from engaging in or continuing any conduct or practice in connection with the purchase or sale of any security, or involving the making of any false filing with the state, entered within five years prior to the filing of the registration statement; or

7) has violated the law of a foreign jurisdiction governing or regulating any aspect of the business of securities or banking or, within the past five years, has been the subject of an action of a securities regulator of a foreign jurisdiction denying, revoking, or suspending the right to engage in the business of securities as a broker-dealer, agent, or investment adviser or is the subject of an action of any securities exchange or self-regulatory organization operating under the authority of the securities regulator of a foreign jurisdiction suspending or expelling such person from membership in such exchange or self-regulatory organization.

B. The prohibitions of Subsections IV.A.1. through 3., and 5. shall not apply if the person subject to the disqualification is duly registered or licensed to conduct securities related business in the state or province in which the administrative order or judgment was entered against such person, or if the broker-dealer employing such person is registered or licensed in the state and the Form B-D filed in the state discloses the order, conviction, judgment, or decree relating to such person.

C. No person disqualified shall act in any capacity other than the capacity for which the person is registered or licensed.

D. Disqualification is automatically waived if the jurisdiction which created the basis for disqualification determines upon a showing of good cause that it is not necessary under the circumstances that registration be denied.

FORM U-1
UNIFORM APPLICATION TO REGISTER SECURITIES

Application to _____ of the
State of _____ pursuant to Section _____
of the _____ .

1. Name and Address of Issuer and principal office in this state:

2. Name, address and telephone number of correspondent to whom notices and communications regarding this application may be sent:

3.Name and address of applicant:

4.Registration or acceptance for filing is sought for the following described securities in the amounts indicated:

Description of Securities	Offering Price or Proposed Offering Price	Total Offering No. of Shares or Units	Amount	Offering in this State No. of Shares or Units	Amount
			$		$
			$		$
			$		$
		Totals	$		$

Indicate the maximum commission to be charged: % _____

5.Amount of filing and examination fees which are enclosed: $ _____

6.A Registration Statement was filed with the Securities and Exchange Commission on_____ and __ became __ will become effective on

_____ .

7.(a) List the states in which it is proposed to offer the securities for sale to the public.

(b) List the states, if any, in which the securities are eligible for sale to the public.

(c) List the states, if any, which have refused, by order or otherwise, to authorize sale of the securities to the public, or have revoked or suspended the right to sell the securities or in which an application has been withdrawn.

8. Submitted herewith as part of this application are the following documents (documents on file may be incorporated by reference):

(a) One copy of the Registration Statement and two copies of the Prospectus in the latest form on file under the Securities Act of 1933.

(b) Underwriting Agreement, Agreement among Underwriters, and Selected Dealers Agreement.

(c) Indenture.

(d) Issuer's charter or articles of incorporation as amended to date.

(e) Issuer's by-laws as amended to date.

(f) Signed copy of opinion of counsel filed with Registration Statement pursuant to the Securities Act of 1933.

(g) Specimen (type of security) _____

(h) Consent to service of process accompanied by appropriate corporate resolution.

(i) If an earning computation or similar requirement is required to be met in this state, attach a separate sheet as an exhibit showing compliance.

(j) One copy of all advertising matter to be used in connection with the offering.

(k) Others (list each): _____

9. The applicant hereby applies for registration or acceptance for filing of the above described securities under the law cited above and in consideration thereof agrees so long as the registration remains in effect that it will:

(a) Advise the above named state authority of any change prior to registration in this state in any of the information contained herein or in any of the documents submitted with or as part of this application.

(b) File with the above named state authority within two business days after filing with the Securities and Exchange Commission (i) any amendments other than delaying amendments to the federal registration statement, designating the changed, revised, or added material or information by underlining the same; and (ii) the final prospectus, or any further amendments or supplements thereto.

(c) Notify the above named state authority within two business days (i) upon the receipt of any stop order, denial, order to show cause, suspension or revocation order, injunction or restraining order, or similar order entered or issued by any state or other regulatory authority or by any court, concerning the securities covered by this application or other securities of the issuer currently being offered to the public; and (ii) upon the receipt of any notice of effectiveness of said registration by the Securities and Exchange Commission.

(d) Notify the above named state authority at least two business days prior to the effectiveness of said registration with the Securities and Exchange Commission of (i) any request by the issuer or applicant to any other state or regulatory authority for permission to withdraw any application to any other state or regulatory authority for permission to withdraw any application to register the securities described herein; and (ii) a list of all states in which applications have been filed where the issuer or applicant has received notice from the state authority that the application does not comply with state requirements and cannot or does not intend to comply with such requirements.

(e) Furnish promptly all such additional information and documents in respect to the issuer or the securities covered by this application as may be requested by the above named state authority prior to registration or acceptance for filing.

U-1 PART 2

Date: _____

_____
(Name of Applicant)

BY: _____
(Name and Title)

STATE OF _____

COUNTY OF _____

The undersigned, _____
being first duly sworn, deposes and says:

That he/she has executed the foregoing application for and on behalf of the applicant named therein; that he/she is _____ of such applicant and is fully authorized to execute and file such application; that he/she is familiar with such application; and that to the best of his/her knowledge, information and belief the statements made in such application are true and the documents submitted therewith are true copies of the originals thereof.

_____
(Name of Applicant)

Subscribed and sworn to before me this _____ day of _____

(Notarial Seal)

_____
                NOTARY PUBLIC

In and for the County of _____ State of _____

My Commission Expires: _____

FOR AN ACKNOWLEDGEMENT OF THE FILING OF THIS
APPLICATION COMPLETE THE FOLLOWING

Name and address of correspondent:

_____

_____

_____

Applicant: _____

Issuer: _____

State of: _____   File Number: _____

Examiner: _____

Telephone: _____

FORM U-7
DISCLOSURE DOCUMENT

> *A manual has been prepared to help you complete this Disclosure Document.*
> *The manual contains instructions for completing each Item. If you do not*
> *have a SCOR Manual, contact your State or Provincial Securities regulator or*
> *the North American Securities Administrators Association.*
>
> THIS BOX IS NOT PART OF THE SCOR FORM AND SHOULD BE REMOVED BEFORE THE
> COMPLETED FORM IS GIVEN TO PROSPECTIVE INVESTORS.

Cover Page - Page I

Place Company Logo (if any) here or to left or right of Company Name

(Exact name of Company as set forth in Articles of Incorporation or Organizational Documents)

Street address of principal office:

Company Telephone Number:
Person(s) to contact at Company with respect to offering:
Telephone Number (if different from above):
Type of securities offered:
Price per security: $
Sales commission, if any: _____%
Minimum number of securities offered:
Maximum number of securities offered:
Total proceeds: If minimum sold: $
               If maximum sold: $

**Investment in a small business is often risky. You should not invest any
funds in this offering unless you can afford to lose your entire investment.
See Item 1 for a discussion of the risk factors that management believes
present the most substantial risks to you.**

The date of this Disclosure Document is _____

Cover Page – Page 2

Executive Summary

The Company

Describe the business of the Company.

Describe how the Company plans to carry out its activities.

This Company:
    [ ] Has never conducted operations.
    [ ] Is in the development stage.
    [ ] Is currently conducting operations.
    [ ] Has shown a profit in the last fiscal year.
    [ ] Other (Specify):

    (Check at least one, as appropriate)

Jurisdiction and date of formation: _____   _____
Fiscal year end: _____   _____
                    (month)   (day)

How the Company Will Use Your Money

Describe how the Company intends to use the proceeds of this offering.

For more information about how the Company will use your money, see Item 30.

The Principal Officers of the Company

The Principal Officers of the Company and their titles are:
    Chief Executive Officer:
    Chief Operating Officer:
    Chief Financial Officer:

For more information about these Officers, see Item 77.

Page – 2

The Offering

Name of Sales Person(s):

Address:

Telephone Number:

Is there an impound of proceeds until the minimum is obtained? [ ] Yes [ ] No
    (See Items 73–76)

Is this offering limited to certain purchasers? [ ] Yes [ ] No (See Item 72)

Is transfer of the securities restricted? [ ] Yes [ ] No (See Item 53)

This offering is available for sale in the following states:

You should consider the terms and risks of this offering before you invest. No government regulator is recommending these securities. No government regulator has verified that this document is accurate or determined that it is adequate. It is a crime for anyone to tell you differently.

The Company has included in this Disclosure Document all of its representations about this offering. If anyone gives you more or different information, you should ignore it. You should rely only on the information in this Disclosure Document.

TABLE OF CONTENTS

RISK FACTORS

1.List in the order of importance the factors that the Company considers to be the most significant risks to an investor.

BUSINESS AND PROPERTIES
GENERAL DESCRIPTION OF THE BUSINESS

2. Describe the business of the Company, including its products or services.

3. Describe how the Company produces or provides these products or services and how and when the Company intends to carry out its activities.

SUPPLIERS

4. Does the Company have any major supply contracts? [ ] Yes [ ] No
If yes, describe.

5. (a) Is the Company dependent upon a limited number of suppliers?
[ ] Yes [ ] No   If yes, describe.

5. (b) Does the Company expect to be dependent upon a limited number of suppliers? [ ] Yes [ ] No   If yes, describe.

CUSTOMER SALES AND ORDERS

6. Does the Company have any major sales contracts? [ ] Yes [ ] No If yes, describe.

7. State the total amount of the Company's sales of products or services for the most recent 12 month financial reporting period.

8. State the dollar amount of a typical sale.

9. Are the Company's sales seasonal or cyclical? [ ] Yes [ ] No If yes, explain.

10. State the amount of foreign sales as a percent of total sales for last fiscal year. _____% Explain the nature of these sales, including any anticipated changes.

11. Name any customers that account for, or based upon existing orders will account for, a major portion (20% or more) of the Company's sales.

12. State the dollar amount of firm orders.

COMPETITION

13. (a) Describe the market area in which the business competes or will compete.

13. (b) Name the Company's principal competitors and indicate their relative size and financial and market strengths.

14. (a) Does the Company compete, or expect to compete, by price?
[ ] Yes [ ] No   If yes, describe its competitive strategy.

14. (b) Does the Company compete, or expect to compete, by service?
[ ] Yes [ ] No   If yes, describe its competitive strategy.

14. (c) Does the Company compete, or expect to compete, on some other basis?
[ ]Yes [ ]No
If yes, state the basis and describe the Company's competitive strategy.

MARKETING

15. (a) Describe how the Company plans to market its products or services during the next 12 months, including who will perform these marketing activities.

15. (b) State how the Company will fund these marketing activities.

EMPLOYEES

16. (a) State the number of the Company's present employees by type of employee (i.e., clerical, operations, administrative, etc.).

16. (b) State the number of employees the Company anticipates it will have within the next 12 months by type of employee (i.e., clerical, operations, administrative, etc.).

17. Describe the Company's labor relations.

18. Indicate any benefits or incentive arrangements the Company provides or will provide to its employees.

PROPERTIES

19. (a) Describe generally the principal properties that the Company owns or leases.

19. (b) Indicate what properties the Company intends to acquire or lease.

RESEARCH AND DEVELOPMENT

20. Indicate the amounts that the Company spent for research and development during its last fiscal year.

21. (a) Will the Company expend funds on research and development during the current fiscal year? [ ] Yes [ ] No

21. (b) If yes, how much does the Company plan to spend on research and development during the current fiscal year?

21. (c) How does the Company intend to fund these research and development costs?

GOVERNMENTAL REGULATION

22. (a) Is the Company's business subject to material regulation by any governmental agency? [ ] Yes [ ] No

22. (b) Are the Company's products or services subject to material regulation by any governmental agency? [ ] Yes [ ] No

22. (c) Are the Company's properties subject to material regulation by any governmental agency? [ ] Yes [ ] No

22. (d) Explain in detail any "yes" answer to Item 22(a), 22(b), or 22(c), including the nature and extent of the regulation and its effect or potential effect upon the Company.

23. (a) Is the Company required to have a license or permit to conduct business? [ ]Yes [ ]No

23. (b) If yes, does the Company have the required license or permit? [ ]Yes [ ]No

23. (c) If the answer to Item 23(b) is "yes," describe the effect on the Company and its business if it were to lose the license or permit.

23. (d) If the Company has not yet acquired a required license or permit, describe the steps the Company needs to take to obtain the license or permit. Estimate the time it will take to complete each step.

COMPANY HISTORY AND ORGANIZATION

24. Summarize the material events in the development of the Company.

25. Describe any recent stock split, stock dividend, recapitalization, merger, acquisition, spin-off, or reorganization.

26. Discuss any pending or anticipated stock split, stock dividend, recapitalization, merger, acquisition, spin-off, or reorganization.

27. State the names of any parent, subsidiary, or affiliate of the Company. For each, indicate its business purpose, its method of operation, its ownership, and whether it is included in the Financial Statements attached to this Disclosure Document.

MILESTONES

28. Describe in chronological order the steps management intends to take to achieve, maintain, or improve profitability during the 12 months following receipt of the offering proceeds.

    If management does not expect the Company to achieve profitability during that time period, describe the business objectives for that period and the steps management intends to take to achieve those objectives.

    Indicate the probable timing of each step and the approximate cost to complete it.

29. (a) State the anticipated consequences to the Company if any step is not completed as scheduled.

29. (b) Describe how the Company will deal with these consequences.

NOTE: After reviewing management's discussion of the steps it intends to take, potential investors should consider whether achievement of each step within the estimated time frame is realistic. Potential investors should also assess the consequences to the Company of any delays in taking these steps and whether the Company will need additional financing to accomplish them.

USE OF PROCEEDS

30. Show how the Company intends to use the proceeds of this offering:

	If Minimum Sold Amount	%	If Maximum Sold Amount	%
Total Proceeds	$	100%	$	100%
Less: Offering Expenses				
Commissions and Finders Fees				
Legal & Accounting				
Copying & Advertising				
Other (Specify):				
Net Proceeds from Offering	$	%	$	%
Use of Net Proceeds				
	$	%	$	%
	$	%	$	%
	$	%	$	%
	$	%	$	%
	$	%	$	%
Total Use of Net Proceeds	$	100%	$	100%

31. (a) Is there a minimum amount of proceeds that must be raised before the Company uses any of the proceeds of this offering? [ ] Yes [ ] No

31. (b) If yes, describe how the Company will use the minimum Net Proceeds of this offering.

31. (c) If the answer to Item 31(a) is "yes," describe how the Company will use the Net Proceeds of this offering that exceed the amount of the minimum offering proceeds.

Page – 13

31. (d) If the answer to Item 31(a) is "no," describe how the Company will use the Net Proceeds of this offering.

32. (a) Will the Company use other funds, together with the offering proceeds, to fund any project or activity identified in Item 31? [ ] Yes [ ] No

32. (b) If yes, state the amounts and sources of the other funds.

32. (c) Indicate whether the availability of the funds is firm or contingent. If contingent, explain.

NOTE: See the answer to Item 70 for information about proceeds used to compensate sales agents. See the answer to Items 108 and 109 for information about proceeds used to purchase assets from Officers, Directors, key persons, or principal stockholders or their associates or to reimburse them for services previously provided or moneys borrowed.

SELECTED FINANCIAL INFORMATION

NOTE: The Company has adjusted all numbers in this section to reflect any stock splits or recapitalizations.

GENERAL

33. What were net, after-tax earnings for the last fiscal year? (If losses, show in parenthesis.)
Total $
Per share $

34. If the Company had profits, show offering price as a multiple of earnings.

$$\frac{\text{Offering Price Per Share}}{\text{Net After-Tax Earnings Per Share for Last Fiscal Year}} = \text{price/earnings multiple}$$

CAPITALIZATION

35. Indicate the capitalization of the Company as of the most recent balance sheet date, and as adjusted to reflect the sale of the minimum and maximum amount of securities in this offering and the use of the net proceeds from this offering.

	Amount Outstanding		
	As of:	As Adjusted	
	/ / (date)	Minimum	Maximum
Debt:			
Short-term debt (average interest rate ____%)	$	$	$
Long-term debt (average interest rate ____%)	$	$	$
Total debt	$	$	$
Stockholders equity (deficit): Preferred stock—par or stated value (by class of preferred - in order of preferences)			
_____	$	$	$
_____	$	$	$
_____	$	$	$
Common stock—par or stated value	$	$	$
Additional paid in capital	$	$	$
Retained earnings (deficit)	$	$	$
Total stockholders equity (deficit)	$	$	$
Total Capitalization	$	$	$

Number of preferred shares authorized to be outstanding:

Class of Preferred	Number of Shares Authorized	Par Value Per Share
		$
		$
		$

Number of common shares authorized: _____ shares.
Par or stated value per share, if any: $ _____

Number of common shares reserved to meet conversion requirements or for issuance upon the exercise of options, warrants or rights: _____ shares.

DILUTION

36. (a) The price of the securities in this offering has been arbitrarily determined.
   [ ]Yes   [ ]No

36. (b) If no, explain the basis on which the price of the securities was determined.

37. (a) The net tangible book value per share before offering is: $

37. (b) For the minimum offering:

   The net tangible book value per share after the
   minimum offering will be: $

   The amount of increase in net tangible book value per share as a
   result of receipt of cash from purchasers in this offering will be: $

   The dilution per share to purchasers will be: $

37. (c) For the maximum offering:
   The net tangible book value per share after the maximum
   offering will be: $

   The amount of increase in net tangible book value per share as a
   result of receipt of cash from purchasers in this offering will be: $

   The dilution per share to purchasers will be: $

38. For each share purchased in this offering a purchaser will pay
   $ _____ but will receive a share representing only $_____ in
   net tangible book value, if the minimum offering is achieved, or
   $ _____, if the maximum offering is achieved.

The difference between the amount a purchaser pays for a share and the amount of net tangible book value that share represents is the dilution to the purchaser.

39. In a table, compare the existing stockholders'percentage ownership in the Company and the consideration paid for that ownership with that of purchasers in this offering.

	Shares Purchased		Total Consideration		Average Price
	Number	Percent	Amount	Percent	Per Share
Existing holders					
New Purchasers:					
Minimum offering					
Maximum offering					

40. Using the offering price of these securities, what value is the Company's management attributing to the entire Company before the offering?
$ _____

NOTE: You should consider carefully whether the Company has this value at the present time. Some issues you should think about include: (1) the risks to which the Company is subject before it achieves success (see Item 1, Risk Factors); (2) the exercise prices of outstanding options (see Item 101); and (3) the prices that the Company's Officers, Directors, and principal stockholders paid for their shares (see Items 104 and 105).

MANAGEMENT'S DISCUSSION AND ANALYSIS OF CERTAIN RELEVANT FACTOR

41. Is the Company having or does the Company anticipate having within the next 12 months any cash flow or liquidity problems? [ ] Yes [ ] No
If yes, explain.

42. (a) Is the Company in default of the terms of any note, loan, lease, or other indebtedness or financing arrangement requiring the Company to make payments? [ ]Yes [ ]No

42. (b) If yes, explain. Identify the creditor, state the amount in default or the term that the Company has not complied with, and describe any consequences to the Company resulting from each default.

43. Are a significant amount of the Company's trade payables more than 90 days old? [ ] Yes [ ] No

44. Is the Company subject to any unsatisfied judgments, liens, or settlement obligations? [ ] Yes [ ] No   If yes, state the amounts.

45. Describe how the Company will resolve the problems identified in Items 41–44.

46. (a) Do the Company's financial statements show losses from operations? [ ]Yes []No

46. (b) If yes, explain the causes underlying these losses and what steps the Company has taken or is taking to address these causes.

47. (a) Describe any trends in the Company's historical operating results.

47. (b) Indicate any changes now occurring in the underlying economics of the Company business which, in the opinion of Management, will have a significant impact upon the Company results of operations within the next 12 months.

47. (c) Describe the probable impact on the Company.

47. (d) Describe how the Company will deal with this impact.

48. (a) Will the proceeds from this offering and any available funds identified in Item 32 satisfy the Company's cash requirements for the 12 month period after it receives the offering proceeds? [ ] Yes [ ] No

48. (b) If no, explain how the Company will satisfy its cash requirements. State whether it will be necessary to raise additional funds. State the source of the additional funds, if known.

DESCRIPTION OF SECURITIES OFFERED
GENERAL

49. The securities being offered are:
    [ ] Common Stock
    [ ] Preferred or Preference Stock
    [ ] Notes, Debentures, or Bonds
    [ ] Limited Liability Company Membership Interests
    [ ] Units of two or more types of securities, composed of:

    [ ] Other (specify):

50. These securities have:
    Yes   No
    [ ]   [ ] Cumulative voting rights
    [ ]   [ ] Other special voting rights
    [ ]   [ ] Preemptive rights to purchase any new issue of shares
    [ ]   [ ] Preference as to dividends or interest
    [ ]   [ ] Preference upon liquidation
    [ ]   [ ] Anti-dilution rights
    [ ]   [ ] Other special rights or preferences (specify):

    Explain any yes answer.

51. Are there any restrictions on dividends or other distributions? [ ] Yes [ ] No
    If yes, describe.

52. Are the securities convertible? [ ] Yes [ ] No
    If yes, state conversion price or formula.

    Date when conversion becomes effective:____/____/___.
    Date when conversion expires: ____/____/___.

53. Describe any resale restrictions on the securities and when the restrictions
    will terminate.

PREFERRED STOCK

If the securities being offered are Preference or Preferred stock:

54. Are unpaid dividends cumulative? [ ] Yes [ ] No

55. (a) Are the securities callable? [ ] Yes [ ] No If yes, describe.

55. (b) Are the securities redeemable? [ ] Yes [ ] No
    If yes, describe, including redemption prices.

DEBT SECURITIES

If the securities being offered are notes or other types of debt securities:

56. What is the interest rate on the debt securities?_____ %
    If the interest rate is variable or there are multiple interest rates, describe.

57. What is the maturity date?____/____/_____

If the securities will have serial maturity dates, describe.

58. Is there a sinking fund? [ ] Yes [ ] No   If yes, describe.

59. Is there a trust indenture? [ ] Yes [ ] No
    If yes, state the name, address, and telephone number of Trustee.

60. (a) Are the securities callable? [ ] Yes [ ]   No If yes, describe.

60. (b) Are the securities redeemable? [ ] Yes [ ] No
    If yes, describe, including redemption prices.

61. Are the securities secured by real or personal property? [ ] Yes [ ] No
    If yes, describe.

62. (a) Are the securities subordinate in right of payment of principal or interest?
    [ ] Yes [ ] No   If yes, explain the terms of the subordination.

62. (b) How much currently outstanding indebtedness of the Company is senior
    to the securities in right of payment of interest or principal? $

63. How much currently outstanding indebtedness ranks equally with the securities in right of payment? $

64. How much currently outstanding indebtedness is junior (subordinated) to the securities? $

RATIO OF EARNINGS TO FIXED CHARGES

65. (a) If the Company had earnings during its last fiscal year, show the ratio of earnings to fixed charges on an actual and pro forma basis for that fiscal year.

	Actual		Pro Forma	
	Last Fiscal Year	Interim Period	Minimum	Maximum
$\dfrac{\text{"Earnings"}}{\text{"Fixed Charges"}} =$				

65. (b) If no earnings, show "Fixed Charges" only

NOTE: See the Financial Statements and especially the Statement of Cash Flows. Exercise care in interpreting the significance of the ratio of earnings to fixed charges as a measure of the "coverage" of debt service. The existence of earnings does not necessarily mean that the Company will have cash available at any given time to pay its obligations. See Items 41–48. Prospective purchasers should not rely on this ratio as a guarantee that they will receive the stated return or the repayment of their principal.

HOW THESE SECURITIES WILL BE OFFERED AND SOLD
COMPANY SALESPERSONS

66. Provide the following information for each Officer, Director, or Company employee who intends to offer or sell the securities:

66.(a)   Name:
          Title:
          Address:

          Telephone Number:

67. Describe any compensation that the Company will pay each person in addition to his or her customary salary and compensation.

OTHER SALESPERSONS AND FINDERS

68. Provide the following information for each salesperson who is not an Officer, Director, or employee of the Company:

68. (a) Name:
          Company:
          Address:

          Telephone Number:

69. Provide the following information for each person who is a finder:

69. (a) Name:
          Company:
          Address:

          Telephone Number:

70. Describe all compensation that the Company will pay to each person identified in Items 68 and 69.

71. Describe any material relationships between these sales persons or finders and the Company or its management.

PURCHASER LIMITATIONS

72. (a) Is the offering limited to certain purchasers? [ ] Yes [ ] No

72. (b) Is the offering subject to any other purchaser limitations? [ ] Yes [ ] No

73. (c) If the answer to either 72(a) or 72(b) is yes, describe the limitation.

IMPOUND OF OFFERING PROCEEDS

73. (a) Will the Company impound the proceeds of the offering until it raises the minimum offering proceeds? [ ] Yes [ ] No

73. (b) If yes, what is the minimum amount of proceeds that the Company must raise and place in an impound account before the Company can receive and use the proceeds?
$

73. (c) If the answer to Item 73(a) is "yes," state the date on which the offering will end if the Company has not raised the minimum offering proceeds.
_____date

74. (a) Does the Company reserve the right to extend the impound period?
[ ]Yes [ ]No

74. (b) If yes, describe the circumstances under which the Company might extend the impound period.

75. State the name, address, and telephone number of the bank or other similar depository institution acting as impound agent.

76. If the offering proceeds are returned to investors at the end of the impound period, will the Company pay any interest earned during the impound period to investors? [ ] Yes [ ] No

MANAGEMENT

OFFICERS AND KEY PERSONS OF THE COMPANY

77. Provide the following information for each Officer and key person. The term "key person" means a person, other than the chief executive officer, chief operating officer, and chief financial officer, makes a significant contribution to the business of the Company. Identify who performs the functions of Chief Executive Officer, Chief Operating Officer, and Chief Financial Officer.

77. (a)   Name:
          Age:
          Title:
          Office Street Address:

          Telephone Number:

Names of employers, titles, and dates of positions held during past five years, with an indication of job responsibilities.

          Education (degrees, schools, and dates):

          Also a Director of the Company [ ] Yes [ ] No

Indicate amount of time to be spent on Company matters if less than full time:

DIRECTORS OF THE COMPANY

78. (a) Number of Directors:

78. (b) Are Directors elected annually? [ ] Yes [ ] No   If no, explain.

78. (c) Are Directors elected under a voting trust or other arrangement?
[ ] Yes [ ] No   If yes, explain.

79. Provide the following information for each Director not described in Item 77:

79. (a)   Name:
          Age:
          Office Street Address:

          Telephone Number:

          Names of employers, titles, and dates of positions held during past five years,
          with an indication of job responsibilities.

          Education (degrees, schools, and dates):

CONSULTANTS

80. (a) Are all key persons employees of the Company? [ ] Yes [ ] No

80. (b) If no, state the details of each contract or engagement.

ARRANGEMENTS WITH OFFICERS, DIRECTORS, AND KEY PERSONS

81. Describe any arrangements to ensure that Officers, Directors, and key per-
    sons will remain with the Company and not compete with the Company if
    they leave.

82. (a) Describe the impact on the Company if it loses the services of any Officer,
    Director, or key person due to death or disability.

82. (b) Has the Company purchased key person life insurance on any Officer, Director, or key person? [ ] Yes [ ] No

82. (c) Has the Company made any arrangements to replace any Officer, Director, or key person it loses due to death or disability? [ ] Yes [ ] No

82. (d) If the answer to either Item 82(b) or 82(c) is "yes," describe.

COMPENSATION

83. List all compensation that the Company paid to its Officers, Directors, and key persons for the last fiscal year:

	Cash	Other
Chief Executive Officer	$	$
Chief Operating Officer		
Chief Financial Officer		
Key Persons:		
Total:	$____	$____
Officers as a group		
(number of persons ____)	$	$
Directors as a group		
(number of persons ____)	$	$
Key Persons as a group		
(number of persons ____)	$	$

84. (a) Has compensation been unpaid in prior years? [ ] Yes [ ] No

84. b) Does the Company owe any Officer, Director, or employee any compensation for prior years? [ ] Yes [ ] No

84. (c) Explain any "yes" answer to Item 84(a) or 84(b).

85. Is compensation expected to change within the next year? [ ] Yes [ ] No If yes, explain.

86. (a) Does the Company have any employment agreements with Officers, Directors, or key persons? [ ] Yes [ ] No   If yes, describe.

86. (b) Does the Company plan to enter into any employment agreements with Officers, Directors, or key persons? [ ] Yes [ ] No   If yes, describe.

PRIOR EXPERIENCE

87. Has any Officer or Director worked for or managed a company (including a separate subsidiary or division of a larger enterprise) in the same type of business as the Company?
[ ] Yes [ ] No   If yes, explain in detail, including relevant dates.

88.(a) If the Company has never conducted operations or is otherwise in the development stage, has any Officer or Director managed another company in the start-up or development stage? [ ]Yes [ ]No

88. (b) If yes, explain in detail, including relevant dates.

CERTAIN LEGAL PROCEEDINGS
Insolvency

89. Has a petition for bankruptcy, receivership, or a similar insolvency proceeding been filed by or against any Officer, Director, or key person within the past five years, or any longer period if material? [ ] Yes [ ] No

90. Was any Officer, Director, or key person an executive of ricer, or in a similar management position for any business entity that was the subject of a petition for bankruptcy, receivership, or similar insolvency proceeding within the past five years, or any longer period if material? [ ] Yes [ ] No

91. Explain in detail any "yes" answer to Item 89 or 90.

Criminal Proceedings

92. (a) Has any Officer, Director, or key person been convicted in a criminal proceeding, excluding traffic violations or other minor offenses? [ ] Yes [ ] No

92. (b) Is any Officer, Director, or key person named as the subject of a pending criminal proceeding, excluding traffic violations or other minor offenses? [ ]Yes [ ]No

 92. (c) Explain in detail any "yes" answer to Item 92(a) or 92(b).

Civil Proceedings

93. (a) Has any Officer, Director, or key person been the subject of a court order, judgment or decree in the last five years related to his or her involvement in any type of business, securities, or banking activity? [ ] Yes [ ] No

93. (b) Is any Officer, Director, or key person the subject of a pending civil or action related to his or her involvement in any type of business, securities, or banking activity? [ ] Yes [ ] No

93. (c) Has any civil action been threatened against any Officer, Director, or key person related to his or her involvement in any type of business, securities, or banking activity? [ ]Yes [ ] No

93. (d) Explain in detail any "yes" answer to Item 93(a), 93(b), or 93(c).

Administrative Proceedings

94. (a) Has any government agency, administrative agency, or administrative court imposed an administrative finding, order, decree, or sanction against any Officer, Director, or key person in the last five years as a result of his or her involvement in any type of business, securities, or banking activity? [ ] Yes [ ] No

94. (b) Is any Officer, Director, or key person the subject of a pending administrative proceeding related to his or her involvement in any type of business, securities, or banking activity? [ ]Yes [ ]No

94. (c) Has any administrative proceeding been threatened against any Officer, Director, or key person related to his or her involvement in any type of business, securities, or banking activity? [ ]Yes [ ]No

94. (d) Explain in detail any "yes" answer to Item 94(a), 94(b), or 94(c).

Self-Regulatory Proceedings

95. (a) Has a self-regulatory agency imposed a sanction against any Officer, Director, or key person in the last five years as a result of his or her involvement in any type of business, securities, or banking activity? [ ] Yes [ ] No

95. (b) Is any Officer, Director, or key person the subject of a pending self-regulatory organization proceeding related to his or her involvement in any type of business, securities, or banking activity? [ ] Yes [ ] No

95. (c) Has any self-regulatory organization proceeding been threatened against any Officer, Director, or key person related to his or her involvement in any type of business, securities, or banking activity? [ ] Yes [ ] No

95. (d) Explain in detail any "yes" answer to Item 95(a), 95(b), or 95(c).

NOTE: After reviewing the background of the Company's Officers, Directors and key persons, potential investors should consider whether or not these persons have adequate background and experience to develop and operate this Company and to make it successful. In this regard, the experience and ability of management are often considered the most significant factors in the success of a business.

OUTSTANDING SECURITIES

GENERAL

96. Describe all outstanding securities.

97. Describe any resale restrictions on outstanding securities and when those restrictions will terminate, if this can be determined.

98. Describe any anti-dilution rights of outstanding securities.

DIVIDENDS, DISTRIBUTIONS, AND REDEMPTIONS

99. (a) Has the Company paid any dividends on its stock, made any distributions of its stock, or redeemed any securities within the last five years? [ ] Yes [ ] No If yes, describe each transaction.

99. (b) Does the Company have any plans or commitments to pay dividends on its stock, make distributions of its stock, or redeem its outstanding securities in the future? [ ] Yes [ ] No   If yes, explain.

OPTIONS AND WARRANTS

100. (a) State the number of shares subject to issuance under outstanding stock purchase agreements, stock options, warrants or rights._____ shares

100. (b) The shares identified in Item 100(a) are _____% of the total shares to be outstanding after the minimum offering.

100. (c) The shares identified in Item 100(a) are_____ % of the total shares to be outstanding after the maximum offering.

101. In a table, describe these stock purchase agreements, stock options, warrants, and rights. State the basic terms of these securities, including the expiration dates, the exercise prices, who holds them, whether they are qualified or non qualified for tax purposes, and whether they have been approved by stockholders.

102. State the number of shares reserved for issuance under existing stock purchase or option plans but not yet subject to outstanding purchase agreements, options, or warrants. shares

103. Does the Company have any plans or commitments to issue or offer options in the future? [ ] Yes [ ] No   If yes, explain.

SALES OF SECURITIES

104. (a) Has the Company sold or issued securities during the last 12 months? [ ]Yes [ ] No

104.(b) If yes, in a table, provide the following information for each transaction: the date of the transaction; the amount and type of securities sold or issued; the number of purchasers to whom the securities were sold or issued; any relationship of the purchasers to the Company at the time of sale or issuance; the price at which the securities were sold or issued; and a concise description of any non-cash consideration.

PRINCIPAL STOCKHOLDERS

105. In the following table, provide the name and office street address of each person who beneficially owns at least 10% of the common or preferred stock of the Company.

Class of Shares	Average Price Per Share	No. of Shares Now Held	% of Total	No. of Shares Held after Offering if All Securities Sold	% of Total

106. Number of shares beneficially owned by all Officers and Directors as a group:

106. (a) Before offering:_____ shares (_____% of total outstanding)

106. (b) After offering:_____ Assuming minimum securities sold: _____ shares (_____% of total outstanding)

106. (c) After offering:_____ Assuming maximum securities sold: _____ shares (_____% of total outstanding)

NOTE: These calculations assume that all outstanding options have been exercised and all convertible securities have been converted.

MANAGEMENT RELATIONSHIPS AND TRANSACTIONS
FAMILY RELATIONSHIPS

107. Is there a family relationship between any Officer, Director, key person, or principal stockholder? [ ] Yes [ ] No   If yes, describe.

MANAGEMENT TRANSACTIONS

108. (a) Will the Company use any offering proceeds to acquire assets from any Officer, Director, key person, or principal stockholder? [ ] Yes [ ] No

108. (b) Will the Company use any offering proceeds to acquire assets from an associate of any Officer, Director, key person, or principal stockholder? [ ] Yes [ ] No

108. (c) If the answer to Item 108(a) or (b) is "yes," provide detailed information about each transaction. Include the name of the person, the cost to the Company, the method used to determine the cost, and any profit to the seller

109. (a) Will the Company use any offering proceeds to reimburse any Officer, Director, key person, or principal stockholder for services already rendered, assets previously transferred, or moneys loaned or advanced, or otherwise? [ ]Yes [ ]No

109. (b) If yes, provide detailed information about each transaction. Include the name of the person, the cost to the Company, the method used to determine the cost, and any profit to the person.

110. (a) Has the Company made loans to any Officer, Director, key person, or principal stockholder within the last two years? [ ] Yes [ ] No

110. (b) Does the Company plan to make loans to its Officers, Directors, key persons, or principal stockholders in the future? [ ] Yes [ ] No

If yes, describe any policies the Company has adopted to deal with the conflicts of interest in these transactions:

111. (a) Has the Company done business with any Officer, Director, key person, or principal stockholder within the last two years? [ ] Yes [ ] No

111. (b) Is the Company currently doing business with any Officer, Director, key person, or principal stockholder? [ ] Yes [ ] No

111. (c) Does the Company plan to do business with its Officers, Directors, key persons, or principal stockholders in the future? [ ] Yes [ ] No

If yes, describe any policies the Company has adopted to deal with the conflicts of interest in these transactions:

112. Explain any "yes" answers to Items 110(a), 111(a), or 111(b). State the principal terms of any significant loans, agreements, leases, financing, or other arrangements.

113. (a) Has any Officer, Director, key person, or principal stockholder guaranteed or co-signed the Company's bank debt or other obligations?
[ ] Yes [ ] No

113. (b) If yes, explain the terms of each transaction and describe the Company's plans for repayment.

LITIGATION

114. Describe any recent or pending litigation or administrative action, which has had or may have a material effect upon the Company's business, financial condition, or operations. State the names of the principal parties, the nature and current status of the matters, and the amounts involved.

115. Describe any threatened litigation or administrative action that may have a material effect upon the Company's business, financial condition, or operations. State the names of the principal parties, and the nature and current status of the matters.

TAX ASPECTS

116. Describe any material tax consequences to investors in this offering.

OTHER MATERIAL FACTORS

117. Describe any other material factors, either adverse or favorable, that will or could affect the Company or its business or which are necessary to make any other information in this Disclosure Document not misleading or incomplete.

ADDITIONAL INFORMATION

118. (a) Describe the types of information that the Company will provide to security holders in the future.

118. (b) Describe the schedule for providing this information.

118. (c) Attach the Company's financial statements to the Disclosure Document.

SIGNATURES:

The Company's Chief Executive Officer, Chief Financial Officer, and its Directors must sign this Disclosure Document. When they sign this Disclosure Document, they represent that they have diligently attempted to confirm the accuracy and completeness of the information in the Document.

When the Chief Financial Officer signs this Disclosure Document, he or she represents that the financial statements in the Document have been prepared in accordance with generally accepted accounting principles, which have been consistently applied, except where explained in the notes to the financial statements. He or she represents that the financial statements fairly state the Company's financial position and results of operations, or receipts and disbursements, as of the dates and periods indicated. He or she also represents that year-end figures include all adjustments necessary for a fair presentation under the circumstances.

Chief Executive Officer: Directors:

_____   _____

Title:_____   _____

Chief Financial Officer: _____

_____   _____

Title:_____   _____

LIST OF EXHIBITS

_____

_____

_____

_____

_____

_____

_____

_____

_____

_____

BIBLIOGRAPHY

Aggarwal, Reena. (2000). "Stabilization Activities by Underwriters after Initial Public Offerings." *Journal of Finance*, 55, 1075–1103.

Aggarwal, Reena. (2002). "Allocation of Initial Public Offerings and Flipping Activity." *Journal of Financial Economics*, 28, 173–208

Aggarwal, Reena, and Patrick Conway. (2000). "Price Discovery in Initial Public Offerings and the Role of the Lead Underwriter." *Journal of Finance*, 55, 2093-2922.

Barber, Brad M., and John D. Lyon. (1997). "Detecting Long-run Abnormal Stock Returns: The Empirical Power and Specification of Test Statistics." *Journal of Financial Economics*, 43, 341–372.

Barry, Christopher B., and Robert H. Jennings. (1993). "The Opening Price Performance of Initial Public Offerings." *Financial Management*, 22, 54–63.

Beatty, Randolph P., and Ivo Welch. (1996). "Issuer Expenses and Legal Liability in Initial Public Offerings." *Journal of Law and Economics*, 39, 545–602.

Benveniste, Lawrence M., and Walid Y. Busaba. (1997). "Bookbuilding vs. Fixed Price: An analysis of Competing Strategies for Marketing IPOs." *Journal of Financial and Quantitative Analysis*, 32, 383–403.

Benveniste, Lawrence M., and Walid Y. Busaba. (1996). "Price Stabilization as a Bonding Mechanism in New Equity Issues." *Journal of Financial Economics*, 42, 223–256.

Bernardo, Antonio E., and Ivo Welch. (2001). "On the Evolution of Overconfidence and Entrepreneurs." *Journal of Economics and Management Strategy*, 10, 301–330.

Booth, James R., and Lena Chua. (1996). "Ownership Dispersion, Costly Information, and IPO Underpricing." *Journal of Financial Economics*, 41, 291–310.

Bradley, Daniel, Brad Jordan, I. Roten, and H. Yi. (2001). "Venture Capital and IPO Lockup Expirations: An Empirical Analysis." Journal of Financial Research, 24, 465–492.

Brav, Alon. (2000). "Inference in Long-Horizon Event Studies: A Bayesian Approach with Applications to Initial Public Offerings." *Journal of Finance*, 55, 1979–2016.

Brav, Alon, and Paul A. Gompers. (1997). "The Long-Run Performance of Initial Public Offerings: What it Takes to Succeed." *Journal of Finance*, 52, 1791–821.

Buser, Stephen A., and K. C. Chan. (1992). *NASDAQ NMS Qualification Standards, Registration Experience and the Price Performance of Initial Public Offerings*. Washington, D.C.: National Association of Securities Dealers, Inc.

Carter, Richard B., Frederick H. Dark, and Alan K. Singh. (1998). "Underwriter Reputation, Initial Returns and the Long-Run Performance of IPO Stocks." *Journal of Finance,* 53, 285–311

Dunbar, Craig G. (2000). "Factors Affecting Investment Bank and Initial Public Offering Share." *Journal of Financial Economics*, 55, 3–41.

Ellis, Katrina, Roni Michaely, and Maureen O'Hara. (2000). "When the Underwriter is the Market Maker: An Examination of Trading in the IPO Aftermarket." *Journal of Finance*, 55, 1039–1074.

Eysell, Thomas H., and Donald R. Kummer. (1993). "Signaling Insider Trading and Post-Offering Performance. The Case of Initial Public Offerings." *Journal of Applied Business Research*, 9, 80–92.

Fama, Eugene. (1991). ''Efflcient Capital Market: II." *Journal of Finance*, 46, 1575–1617

Field, Laura C., and Gordon Hanka. (2001). 'The Expiration of IPO Share Lockups." *Journal of Finance*, 56, 471–500.

Garfinkel, Jon A. (1993). "Valuation of an Initial Public Offering." *Financial Management*, 22, 74–83.

Habib, Michael, and Alexander Ljungqvist. (2001). "Underpricing and Entrepreneurial Wealth Losses in IPOs: Theory and Evidence." *Review of Financial Studies*, 14, 433–458.

Hanley, Kathleen Weiss. (1993). "The Underpricing of Initial Public Offerings and the Partial Adjustment Phenomenon." *Review of Financial Studies*, 34, 231–250.

Hensler, Douglas A., Ronald C. Rutherford, and Thomas M. Springer. (1997). "The Survival of Initial Public Offerings in the Aftermarket." *Journal of Financial Research*, 20, 93–110.

Jain, B. A. (1997). "Tests of Adverse Selection Models in the New Issues Market." *Omega*, 25, 365–376.

Jenkinson, Tim, and Alexander Ljungqvist. (2001) *Going Public: The Theory and Evidence on How Companies Raise Equity Finance* (2nd edition). New York: Oxford University Press.

Kaplan, Charles J. (1997). "Initial Public Offerings—The Tendency to Underperform the Market." *http//www.ipoalley.com/ipo/bplan9.htm.*

Kaplan, Robert S., and David P. Norton. (1996). *The Balanced Scorecard.* Cambridge, MA: Harvard Business Press.

Kim, Moonchul, and Jay R. Ritter. (1999). "Valuing IPOs." *Journal of Financial Economics*, 53, 409–437.

Krigman, L., W. Shaw, and K. Womack. (1999). "The Persistence of IPO Mispricing and the Predictive Power of Flipping." *Journal of Finance,* 54, 1015-1044.

Latane, Henry A., and Charles P. Jones. (1997). "IPO: Using a Forward-Thinking Approach." *Journal of Finance*, 32, 1457–1465.

Lee, Philip J., Stephen L. Taylor, and Terry S. Walter. (1999). "IPO Underpricing Explanations: Implications for Investor and Allocation Schedules." *Journal of Financial and Quantitative Analysis*, 34, 425–444.

Leedy, Paul D. (1997). *Practical planning and design of an IPO.* Englewood Cliffs, NJ: Simon & Schuster.

Lerner, Josh. (1994). "Venture Capitalists and the Decision to go Public." *Journal of Financial Economics*, 35, 293–316.

Levin, Richard I., and David S. Rubin. (1991). *Statistics for Management.* Englewood Cliffs, NJ: Prentice Hall.

Loughran, Tim, and Jay R. Ritter. (1995). "The IPO Puzzle." *Journal of Finance*, 50, 23–51.

Lyon, John D., Brad M. Barber, and Chih-Ling Tsai. (1999). "Improved Methods for Tests of Long-Run Abnormal Stock Returns." *Journal of Finance*, 54,165–201.

Maksimovic, Vojislav, and Pegaret Pichler. (2001). "Technological Innovation and Initial Public Offerings." *Review of Financial Studies*, 14, 459–494.

Mello, Antonio, and John Parsons. (1998). "Going Public and the Ownership Structure of the Firm." *Journal of Financial Economics*, 49, 79–109.

Michaely, Roni, and Wayne H. Shawl (1994). "The Pricing of Initial Public Offerings: Test of Adverse-Selection and Signaling Theories." *Review of Financial Studies*, 7, 279–319.

Miller, Robert E., and Frank K. Reily. (1997). "An Examination of Mispricing, Returns and Uncertainty for Initial Public Offerings." *Financial Management*, 16, 33–71.

Muscarella, Chris J., and Michael Vetsuypens.(1998). "The Underpricing of Second Initial Public Offerings." *Journal of Financial Research*, 12, 173–192.

Rajan, Raghuram, and Henri Servaes. (1997). "Analyst Following of Initial Public Offerings." *Journal of Finance*, 52, 507–529.

Reily, Frank K., and Edgar A. Norton. (1996). *Investments*. Fort Worth, TX: Dryden Press.

Ritter, Jay R. (1995). "The Long-Run Performance of Initial Public Offerings." *Journal of Finance*, 46, 3–38.

Spatt, Chester, and Sanjay Srivastava. (1991). "Preplay Communication, Participation Restrictions, and Efficiency in Initial Public Offerings." *Review of Financial Studies*, 4, 709–726.

Spiess, Katherine D., and Richard H. Pettway. (1997). "The IPO Process of Obtaining Long-Run Success." *Journal of Banking and Finance*, 21, 967-988.

Stoughton, Neal M., and Josef Zechner. (1998). "IPO Mechanisms, Monitoring and Ownership Structure." *Journal of Financial Economics*, 45, 45–77.

Teoh, Siew Hoong, Ivo Welch, and T. J. Wong. (1998). "Earnings Management and the Long-Run Market Performance of Initial Public Offerings of Common Stock." *Journal of Finance*, 53, 1935–1974.

Ward's Business Directory. (1999). New York: Information Access Company.

Zikmund, William G. (1997). *Business Research Methods*. Fort Worth, TX: Dryden Press.

INDEX

D

E

About TEXERE

Texere, a progressive and authoritative voice in business publishing, brings to the global business community the expertise and insights of leading thinkers. Our books educate, enlighten, and entertain, and provide an intersection where our authors and our readers share cutting edge ideas, practices, and innovative solutions. Texere seeks to cultivate, enhance, and disseminate information that illuminates the global business landscape.

www.thomson.com/learning/texere

About the Typeface

This book was set in 11.5 point Times New Roman. Times New Roman was created in 1931 by Stanley Morison of London, England. This typeface is known for its strength of line, firmness of contour and economy of space.

Library of Congress Cataloging-in-Publication Data

Kleeburg, Richard P.
  Initial public offering / by Richard P. Kleeburg.
      p. cm.
  Includes bibliographical references and index.
  ISBN 0-324-20056-0 (hardcover : alk. paper)
  1. Going public (Securities) I. Title.
  HG4028.S7K546 2005
  658.15'224--dc22
>   2005001440